THE DEBT CURE

CENTENNIAL BOOKS

THE DEBT CURE

175 PROVEN STRATEGIES FOR FINANCIAL INDEPENDENCE

TAYLOR SMITH

CENTENNIAL BOOKS

Table of Contents

120

28

164

158

Debt 101

Defining debt, who takes it on—and
why do we have so much of it?

Debt provides opportunities,
but if you don't handle it
carefully, you can have
difficulties staying afloat.

WHAT IS DEBT? Understanding the term, how to manage it and the best ways to pay it off

Let's face it: Debt is in our nature. Humans have been borrowing and lending valuable items for ages. In fact, some of the earliest surviving examples of written language are essentially purchase orders and receipts, records of who owed what to whom.

But when we talk about debt today, what do we mean? Put simply, debt is money owed. The debts we hold today are mortgages and car loans. They're credit card balances and student loans, and even debts owed to the government. And like many Americans, your debt can include some or all of the above.

For many of us, debt is a useful tool. It gives us financial flexibility and allows us to purchase big items. But if it's not handled carefully, debt can be difficult to overcome. That's why it's important to make smart choices around debt, from understanding how interest rates work to learning the best ways to dig yourself out of mounting credit card debt.

> It's important to make smart choices around debt, from understanding how interest rates work to learning the best ways to dig yourself out of credit card debt.

Why Debt Can Get the Better of You

Two aspects of debt can make it risky. First, you are making a good-faith promise to repay what you owe with money you expect to receive in the future—and the future is uncertain. You could lose your job or face some other financial obligation that keeps you from working. Second, if you fall behind on your interest payments—the additional money paid on most loans—your debt only gets bigger and more difficult to pay off. That can cause real problems over time.

How to Manage Debt

It's not always a bad idea to take on debt. Financially responsible people take out student loans, auto loans, mortgages—even second mortgages—all the time. And no one expects you *not* to have an energy bill. But debt needs to be managed. The first, best step is to limit the size of your debt.

A simple way to determine a sustainable debt level is to find your debt-to-income (DTI) ratios. There are two types of DTI: front-end and back-end. Your front-end DTI is the percentage of your gross income that is spent on recurring housing debts such as monthly rent or mortgage payments. Your back-end DTI is the percentage of your gross income that is spent on all debt payments, including student loans, auto loans, credit cards and child support or alimony. Recurring expenses from bills like auto insurance or utilities don't count.

Consider your job security, family plans and lifestyle to determine how much debt you can comfortably afford.

Lenders may look at both your DTI ratios to determine whether it's a good bet to loan you money, and their standards can be used as a guide. Often lenders look for a back-end DTI of 36% or lower. A good front-end DTI is 28% or lower, although the back-end DTI is often more important to lenders.

After looking at your DTI, you'll want to consider things like your job security, your family plans and your lifestyle to determine how much debt you can comfortably afford.

Paying Off Debt

If you find your debt getting away from you, the solution almost always involves lifestyle changes. Put simply, it means figuring out how to spend less or earn more. What extras can you do without while you put more money toward your credit card or mortgage? Can you find some creative ways to boost your income and supercharge your debt payments?

Meanwhile, there are ways to reduce your monthly payments to make them more manageable. You may be able to consolidate multiple debts into a single loan, or refinance by replacing a current loan with a new one at a lower monthly payment. That can often mean increasing the term of the loan and, ultimately, paying more in interest. You can also look into using a credit card balance transfer to move a balance to a new account at a different company at a lower interest rate.

Prioritize debts with the highest interest rates and the worst consequences for default. Don't be afraid to call your creditors and tell them about your situation. You may be surprised to find that they're willing to work with you and help you find a way out of debt.

PRO TIP

Prioritize your debts so you start by targeting those with the highest interest rates and the worst consequences if you go into default.

Studies show that people spend more when using credit over cash—so be careful about always pulling out that card.

SECURED VS. UNSECURED DEBT How to tell the difference between these two types of debt—and why it matters

Mortgages, student loans, credit cards and car payments are all examples of debt, yet each functions a little bit differently. One of the main ways they differ is whether or not the lender requires you to provide collateral—an asset that functions as a backup for your loan in case you default. This distinction can help you understand whether debt is secured or unsecured. It also can help you learn how particular loans function, and decide how to prioritize paying off your debts.

Secured Debt

Secured debts are backed—or secured—by an asset that acts as collateral for a loan. With a secured loan, your payment is directly tied to this asset. The lender, or lien holder, is legally allowed to seize the asset and use it to pay your debt if you miss a certain number of payments.

Let's say you've taken out a loan to purchase your house, and you've agreed to make monthly mortgage payments of a specified amount. If you become delinquent, or even default on your loan by missing too many payments, the lender may decide to start foreclosure proceedings, which means they will repossess your house, kicking you out in the process. The same goes for your car: If you neglect your monthly auto payments long enough, the lender can seize your vehicle. (Ever

Secured loans require you to provide collateral that your lender can seize if you don't make payments.

heard of the repo man? That's where he comes in—showing up at your house to literally repossess, or take back, your car.)

In both cases, the lender has the right to sell the assets to recover some of the money they're owed—and if the sale doesn't cover the entire debt, you may have to pay the difference.

With any secured debt, you don't completely own the asset until you've paid off the loan in full. Once you pay it off, however, you can ask the lender to

Not paying your credit card bill can hurt your credit score and make it harder to get loans in the future.

provide a new title for the asset, thereby "releasing" it—meaning it's yours forever, or at least until you decide to sell.

Secured debts are typically easier for borrowers to obtain because the collateral makes them less risky for lenders to issue. These types of loans are extremely important to repay, because defaulting on a secured loan could mean losing your shelter, transportation or another important asset.

Unsecured Debt

Unsecured debts are not tied to a particular asset, which makes them riskier for lenders. To balance that higher risk, lenders make borrowers pay more in interest. And while you may not have your house taken away from you for missed payments, defaulting on unsecured debts can have consequences.

Credit cards, student loans and personal loans are all examples of unsecured debt, as are medical bills and court-ordered child support. If you default, you may be subject to late fees and other penalties. Fail to pay too long and your lender will likely take measures to collect payment, including hiring a debt collector, asking the court to garnish your wages or putting a lien on an asset until you pay. The lien is

your lender's way of staking their claim to your asset, and it prevents you from selling it, transferring ownership or using it to secure other debt.

For example, if you rack up a large credit card balance and don't pay it in full each month, the balance will continue to grow, accruing interest on top of the original amount owed. If you stop paying the bill, the credit card company might turn your account over to collections. Debt collectors will contact you any way they can—phone, email, maybe even showing up in person—to arrange a payment plan.

Your lender can also report your delinquent status to the credit-reporting bureaus (Experian, Equifax and TransUnion). These organizations track your debt information and compile the credit score that lenders use to determine whether to give you a loan. While timely unsecured debt payments can improve your credit score, missed payments and delinquency can hurt your credit score. A low score makes it harder to get the best loan terms from lenders, and may even keep lenders from giving you a loan.

PRO TIP

Unsecured debts are more risky for lenders, so you're likely to pay more in interest on these loans than you would on a secured loan.

13

WHAT KINDS OF DEBT DO WE OWE? A look at the common categories of debt Americans encounter

Almost everyone borrows money at one time or another, and it's not uncommon to hold several types of debt at once. But not all debt is created equal. People use debt for many purposes, and creditors and the IRS can treat various types of debt differently. The type of debt will also determine the effect it will have on your credit score.

Debt can be broken down into two broad categories: installment debt and revolving debt. Installment debt is meant for specific purposes and is paid back over a set period of time. Installment debt allows you to borrow money to pay for an expensive item or service that you otherwise wouldn't be able to afford. This kind of debt often comes with potential tax deductions, and, as long as you make regular payments, doesn't negatively affect your credit score.

> People use debt for many purposes, and creditors and the IRS can treat various types of debt differently.

Examples of Installment Debt

• **Mortgages** Mortgages are used to buy homes, rental properties or other kinds of real estate. Banks typically issue loans with payoff schedules that last 15 or 30 years. That allows them to offer relatively low monthly payments, as well as lower interest rates than other consumer loan products. Most taxpayers can also deduct the interest they pay on their mortgage.

• **Auto Loans** Auto loans generally have a term between 36 and 72 months. In most cases, you borrow a lump sum from a bank (even if you get your financing through a car dealer) and pay it back with interest over time. The loan amount doesn't have to equal the full value of the car. For example, you may be able to offset the price by trading in your old vehicle or making a down payment.

• **Student Loans** If you've had to pay for higher education, you're likely familiar with federal and private student loans. Federal loans are issued by the government, and have relatively low interest rates and offer fixed rates for new borrowers. Private loans come from banks and other private lenders who set the interest rates and conditions of the loan. Taking out a student loan is an investment in education, typically with the hope that it will pay off in the form of a higher-paying job. And the interest you pay on student loans is often tax-deductible.

• **Personal Loans** Unlike mortgages, auto loans or student loans, personal loans can be used for a variety of major expenses. For example, you might take out a personal loan to do a home renovation, take a once-in-a-lifetime trip, move across the country or invest in a small business. Personal loans generally are not tax-deductible.

- **Medical Debt** Many medical providers offer payment plans to help you afford specific medical treatments or procedures. Those that don't accept payment plans will sometimes offer medical credit cards, which often come with interest-free periods of up to a year.

- **Tax Debt** If you're unable to pay your taxes in full by the filing deadline, you'll owe the IRS money in the form of tax debt. You can arrange a repayment schedule with the IRS.

Revolving debt, on the other hand, is taken on for no specific purpose and has no repayment time line—meaning it can last indefinitely. The most common example is credit card debt. If you carry a high amount of revolving debt relative to the amount of credit available to you, your credit score may suffer.

Examples of Revolving Debt

- **Credit Card Debt** You incur credit card debt when you don't pay off your monthly credit card bill in full. Interest rates vary dramatically, depending on your credit history and the overall interest rate environment, as well as what type of card you carry. For instance, store-specific credit cards often charge higher rates than your average Mastercard or Visa. It's possible to rack up debt on multiple credit cards at once.

- **Home Equity** A home equity line of credit, or HELOC, is a type of revolving credit that uses your home as collateral. Like credit cards, HELOCs can be used to pay for all sorts of expenses. Since long-term failure to repay a HELOC may result in the loss of your home, they should only be taken out if you are certain you can repay.

If you can't pay your taxes by the filing deadline, you'll have to arrange a repayment schedule with the IRS.

DEBT BY THE NUMBERS How much do we owe? And where does all that debt come from?

The average monthly car payment for a new vehicle is $550.

At the end of 2019, American household debt topped $14 trillion. That's a big number, but what does it really mean? The average household owes roughly $137,000 in total debt from sources like mortgages, credit card balances and more.

Those averages don't quite tell the whole story, however. For one thing, not everybody has a mortgage. Most of us do have credit cards, though—2.5 credit cards per American, as a matter of fact. And for the past few years, in addition to putting more purchases on our cards, we've been taking out more car and school loans, too. If you're in debt in America, you're not alone.

Home Is Where the Mortgage Is

Nearly $9.5 trillion of American's collective household debt takes the form of mortgages, making up about 70% of total household debt. To put that in perspective, we owe more than twice as much in mortgages as we do for all other types of loans combined.

Housing debt has risen over the past few years, but is still well below the peak we saw in 2008 during the financial crisis. The good news: Homeowners are staying on top of their mortgage payments, and default rates have fallen in recent years. One reason may be that lenders have been pickier about who gets new loans.

Interest rates have for the most part declined recently, but how they'll change in the future is anybody's guess. For now, mortgage rates remain relatively low by historical standards. So if you're planning to pay down your total debt, focus on higher-interest loans like credit cards first before you put more money toward your mortgage.

Credit Cards: The Elephant in the Room

After accounting for the mortgage portion of the debt Americans owe, we're left with about $4.5 trillion in consumer debt. Around a fifth of that debt is tied to credit card accounts. As of early 2020, the average account had a balance of about $6,200.

While some households routinely pay those balances off, about four in 10 U.S. households carry a monthly balance from month to month. Many of those households have roughly $7,000 to $8,000 in outstanding balances. And if their cards have high interest rates, paying those balances down can be even more difficult.

> **PRO TIP**
> The average U.S. household owes roughly $136,000 in total debt from sources ranging from mortgages to credit card balances.

We're also putting more of our everyday purchases on our cards these days. The total amount of

> The typical American holds four different credit cards, according to credit bureau Experian, giving us a lot of room to accrue debt.

credit card debt in the United States has risen 28% over the past five years. According to Experian, a consumer credit reporting agency, our total card balances went up about 6% between 2018 and 2019 alone.

But the rise in outstanding card debt doesn't necessarily mean more consumers are falling into financial trouble. The fact is, we're using our debit and credit cards more than ever, choosing to swipe a card at the checkout counter rather than count out bills for the cashier. What's more, many consumers also choose to use their credit cards instead of cash to take advantage of rewards such as cash back or travel miles.

Rising Student and Auto Loan Balances

Even though we're carrying more credit card debt these days, those debts have actually shrunk as a percentage of our overall household debt. That's because we've taken on a lot more debt from other places.

Non-revolving debt is the catchall bucket for money we owe that's not on a credit card or a mortgage. For the most part, it's made up of student loans and auto loans, and borrowing has increased in both categories over the past decade.

Auto loans: In recent years, buyers have snapped up more cars, as low interest rates made new loans more attractive to consumers. As a result, the number of new auto loans has now risen for nine consecutive years. By the end of 2019, Americans owed more than $1.2 trillion in auto loan debt.

Student loans: Student-loan debt has risen more than 150% in the past decade, to more than $1.56 trillion. That's over $500 billion more than our total credit card debt, and it's spread across many fewer borrowers. Students who graduated with

Student-loan debt has risen more than 150 percent in the past decade.

debt in 2018 took on an average of about $35,000 in loans, which works out to an average monthly student-loan payment of $402. According to researchers, over half of the students who graduate with student debt probably won't pay off their loans until after they turn 40 years old.

Debt Is Neither Good nor Bad

Taking on debt isn't necessarily a bad decision. Educational loans give you an opportunity to learn, which could lead to a better career and more financial stability. Credit cards give you the flexibility to pay off big purchases over time. Taking on too much debt can lead to financial woes, of course. But when used in moderation, debt can open up new opportunities and offer some financial flexibility, which can help make your day-to-day life a little easier.

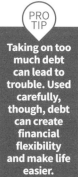

PRO TIP

Taking on too much debt can lead to trouble. Used carefully, though, debt can create financial flexibility and make life easier.

DEBT BY GENERATION Why baby boomers, Gen Xers and millennials feel differently about debt

C ertain events loom large in a generation's collective memory, and those events often influence their opinions, including how they feel about debt.

For example, the Great Recession struck when millennials were in their teens and 20s, shaping the generation's impressions of the banking industry and spurring them to become highly cautious spenders. Baby boomers, on the other hand, took out student loans just like millennials did, but got higher-paying jobs out of school, paid off their loans much faster and have a much brighter outlook on debt and the financial system.

Here's a breakdown of each generation's outlook on debt.

Baby boomers look much more positively on debt than millennials do.

Baby Boomers

The baby boom generation, now in their mid-50s to early 70s, took on more debt than the previous generation—in part because of their desire for large homes and higher-end cars. Most see those loans as necessary tools that helped them achieve their dreams—whether multiple degrees, a big house in the suburbs or a shiny Mercedes-Benz in the driveway.

Baby boomers went to college at a time when tuition costs were much lower than today. What's more, their college degrees often helped them secure well-paying jobs. Taking out student loans

typically paid off for boomers, and they continued to use debt as a part of their financial tool kit as they progressed through their careers.

Now that they're reaching retirement, boomers are carrying much more mortgage debt than their parents were at the same age. In fact, Americans over 60 are three times as likely to still be repaying home loans than they were in 1980.

Even though some baby boomers will be paying off mortgages for the rest of their lives, this generation has an overall positive outlook on debt.

The Great Recession has left millennials more risk-averse than previous generations when it comes to debt.

Generation X

Compared to boomers, Generation X have had a different relationship with debt from the start. Gen Xers, who are in their late 30s through their early 50s, have the highest debt load of any generation, and feel deeply burdened by it. The average Gen Xer owes more than $30,000 in non-mortgage debt—more than any other generation.

A few factors explain Gen X's debt load: First, members of this age group spent heavily as they tried to keep up with boomers. Many are now saddled with care expenses for young children and aging parents. And many were buying homes just before the housing bubble burst.

Members of Gen X aren't optimistic about their ability to repay their debts. More than one in five Gen Xers believe they might never pay it all off.

Millennials

Known as the most risk-averse generation, millennials, who are between their early 20s and late 30s, are the least likely generation to see debt as a tool to enhance their lifestyle.

Although the Great Recession came before most millennials were starting to build their wealth, the event still affected their views of both the financial industry and debt. Witnessing how the financial crisis affected their elders—sometimes their own family members—made many millennials be much more cautious with their own money. The recession also affected millennials as they entered the job market and struggled to find well-paying employment.

Despite their mistrust of banks and wariness of debt, millennials haven't avoided taking out loans altogether. In fact, more millennials carry student-loan debt than previous generations, and they owe higher balances. Though college-educated millennials have secured higher-paying work than their peers without college degrees, huge student-loan payments and stagnant wages have led some millennials to put off buying homes and having children.

WHY DO WE TAKE ON DEBT? From financial strategizing to living beyond their means, the reasons Americans go into debt

Americans take on debt for all kinds of reasons. Some debts can be a drag on your finances, while others function as an important part of a healthy financial plan. For most people, buying a home requires getting a mortgage. Or, if you're attending college, it likely means taking out student loans. In both cases, taking on this debt is strategic. You expect that your investment—whether in a home or an education—will pay off in the future.

It's a reasonable expectation: The average worker with a bachelor's degree can expect to earn 66% more over their lifetime than someone with only a high school degree. And average income levels continue to rise with more advanced degrees. Likewise, though a home is often the biggest purchase a person will make during their lifetime, most homebuyers are willing to take on a mortgage because they'd rather put monthly housing payments toward something they believe will appreciate in value and that they'll own outright at the end of the loan.

People also take on debt as a way to build credit. For example, by signing up for a credit card and making your payments on time, you demonstrate to potential lenders that you are a responsible borrower. Building credit helps boost your credit score, making you eligible for larger lines of credit and better interest rates down the line. Many credit cards also offer perks like airline miles and cash back. These cards often carry higher interest rates, so using them can pay off—provided you pay your balance in full each month.

Building credit helps boost your credit score, which makes you eligible for more credit at better rates.

Debt can range from necessary expenses like housing and food to optional purchases like air travel.

PRO TIP

Take on strategic debt (like a student loan or a mortgage) when you expect the investment you're funding to pay off in the future.

23

The Downside of Debt

The problem comes when we take on debt we can't pay off. This often happens when we rack up credit card debt. As interest accrues on our outstanding balance, the debt becomes more and more difficult to pay off. Most credit cards function on a system of compound interest—the amount you owe often grows even while you're paying off your balance.

More than 40% of all U.S. households carry some sort of credit card debt, with an average balance of around $7,000. While that's not an impossible sum to pay off, many cardholders pay only the minimum each month (generally less than 4% of the total owed). But making only the minimum payment will take you more than 20 years to pay off that $7,000 balance. Not only that, the amount you will have paid in interest over the course of those 20 years will have far exceeded the amount you originally charged to your card.

Over time, what may have started out as a $7,000 living room set turns into a $16,000 expense that you're still paying off long after you've sold all your old furniture at a yard sale. This system of compound interest and minimum monthly payments can make it difficult to pay off debts—especially if you've charged more than you can actually afford.

Living Outside Our Means

More than half of all Americans report spending more money than they make. This overspending may be a result of splurging on too many restaurant meals or spending too much on clothes and housewares to keep up with the neighbors.

Yet many Americans actually will find themselves in debt due to income volatility—defined as fluctuations in income of at least 25% year over year. More than a third of U.S. families experience these dramatic swings in income, which make it difficult to create budgets and pay off bills on time. This volatility can also make it difficult to cover emergencies when they arise. Even with insurance, accidents and unexpected health issues leave many people saddled with thousands of dollars in medical debt.

For most people,
buying a home
requires a mortgage.

Understanding Debt

Everything you need to know about
loans, interest rates and credit
scores—and why not all debt is bad

ALL ABOUT INTEREST RATES Why lenders charge them, how they work and how they affect you

"**B**uy now and take advantage of low interest rates!" We hear this type of sales pitch all the time, but what does it really mean? The fact is, interest rates matter when it comes to loans. An interest rate is the proportion of a loan that a lender charges a borrower. Think of it as the fee you pay for taking out a loan, or taking advantage of credit. It's also the way that lenders make their money.

When you take out a personal loan or make purchases with a credit card, the amount of interest you pay is based on the loan or the card's interest rate. These rates vary depending on the perceived risk of the borrower, which largely depends on the borrower's credit rating. These days, people with excellent credit ratings can expect an interest rate of about 10% on a personal loan, while those with poor credit ratings face interest rates pushing 30%.

The lower the interest rate, the less you'll pay over the life of a loan.

PRO TIP

A high credit score can help you land the best interest rates. One way to keep your score up is to make sure your bills are paid on time.

But interest rates work in the opposite direction, too. When you put money in a savings account, you're lending a bank money, and the amount of interest you receive is based on the account's interest rate. These rates are typically quite low compared to the interest rates on personal loans or credit cards: In 2019, they were about 0.09% on average.

Interest rates make the headlines in the U.S. on a fairly regular basis. When this happens, it's usually because the Federal Reserve has changed—or may be changing—the federal funds rate. This is the rate that banks charge each other to lend Federal Reserve funds overnight. While it may not seem like the most important figure in the world, the federal funds rate actually has a huge effect on the interest rates charged to individuals and businesses, which in turn has a significant impact on national economic growth.

Here's a closer look at interest rates and how they affect both your personal finances and the broader economy.

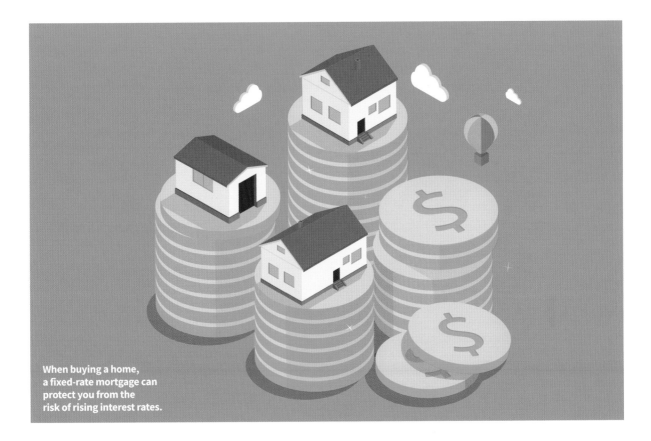

When buying a home, a fixed-rate mortgage can protect you from the risk of rising interest rates.

Fixed vs. Variable Rates

A fixed interest rate is established at the outset of a loan and doesn't change over time. A variable interest rate, meanwhile, can go up or down depending on market fluctuations. Many types of loans, including personal loans, mortgages and private student loans, give you a choice between fixed and variable interest rates. Other loans, such as auto loans, almost always come with a fixed rate.

Fixed-rate loans are attractive to many people because they are more predictable and can be budgeted more easily. In particular, if you're planning to take a long time to pay back a loan—say a decade or longer—a fixed rate can help protect you against the risk of rising interest rates. Variable-rate loans may be preferable if their initial rates are lower and you expect to pay off the loan within a shorter time frame.

Variable-rate loans are typically tied to an index such as the London Interbank Offered Rate, or LIBOR, which is a rate at which many global banks borrow from one another. The frequency with which the rate of a variable-rate loan is updated differs from loan to loan. It may change monthly, quarterly or annually, for example. Many variable-rate loans have a cap, or an upper limit on the rate you can be charged, no matter how much the underlying index rises.

Most people considering a student loan must choose between federal loans, which have fixed rates, and private loans, which often have variable rates. Interest rates on federal student loans are determined by Congress each year. Private student loans may come with lower initial rates for candidates with good credit, making them more attractive for some borrowers who plan to pay off their loans relatively quickly.

APR: What Is It—And Why Does It Matter?

APR stands for annual percentage rate. It's the kind of interest rate that you'll get with most credit cards and consumer loans. APRs remain the same over the course of each year, although some may be subject to changes from year to year. They are not to be confused with annual percentage yields, or APYs, which are the interest rates you earn from putting money in a savings account or certificate of deposit (CD).

Credit card APRs are probably the most common form of this kind of interest rate. Many credit cards apply different APRs to the different ways you can use your card. For example, APRs for cash advances are typically higher than the APRs for purchases. In addition, many credit cards offer a low introductory APR for the first several months you use it.

How and Why Interest Rates Change

Interest rates vary from loan to loan and person to person, but most interest rates are based on a rate set by the country's central bank. In the U.S., the federal funds rate is set by the U.S. Federal Reserve. The Fed reviews it eight times per year, and decides whether to raise it, lower it or keep it the same. This rate affects the rates banks offer to consumers and businesses.

Lower interest rates tend to encourage borrowing, since the cost to borrowers is lower. They also encourage higher spending and riskier investing, which gives businesses more money to put toward growth initiatives. The net result is often economic expansion.

But low interest rates, over time, can cause demand to exceed supply, which may result in an undesirable rate of inflation. To correct for this imbalance, the central bank may raise interest rates for a while. We saw this happen in 2018, when the Federal Reserve raised interest rates four times during a period of widespread economic growth. These higher interest rates encouraged people to borrow less and save more, leading to slower economic growth. In response to this slowed growth, the Fed then lowered interest rates repeatedly throughout 2019.

The Effect of Interest Over Time

When you're just paying a small chunk of interest every month, it may not seem very consequential in terms of your overall finances. But those small chunks eventually add up over time, and over the course of a year—or a decade— too much interest can really prevent you from achieving your desired lifestyle.

This is especially true if some or all of your interest is compound, rather than simple, interest. Simple interest applies only to the amount of the loan, which is known as the principal. Compound interest applies both to the amount of the loan as well as to the accumulated interest on that loan. As a result, loans that have compound interest are typically more expensive than those with simple interest.

For example, let's say you took out a $20,000 loan with an interest rate of 10% for a three-year period. Calculating this under the simple interest method, you'd owe $6,000 in interest for the length of the loan. Under the compound interest method, you'd owe $6,964 when the interest is compounded monthly. It's also important to remember that the longer the time frame to pay off the loan, the greater the negative effect that compound interest has.

> Small interest payments add up over time. Over the course of a year—or a decade—too much interest can prevent you from achieving your desired lifestyle.

For richer or poorer? Married couples should carefully weigh which debts to share and which to keep separate.

PRO TIP

Check the terms of your loan to see how interest is calculated. Over time, compound interest will cost more than simple interest.

When you're the one lending the money, of course, compound interest works in your favor. Almost all savings accounts and CDs give you compound interest on your savings, albeit at lower rates than you'd pay to take a loan from the same bank. The difference between these two figures—the rate the bank pays you and the rate you pay the bank—accounts for the profits earned by the bank. Small interest payments add up over time. Over the course of a year—or a decade—too much interest can prevent you from achieving your desired lifestyle.

WHO'S RESPONSIBLE FOR DEBT? **The answer usually depends on who signed the paperwork, but inheriting debt is another story**

Who's responsible for what debt can get complicated. If your son can't make his student loan payments, are you on the hook? What about your spouse's shopping habits—do you have to pay his or her outstanding credit card balance? What happens when a loved one dies, leaving an unpaid mortgage behind?

In each case, the answers depend on the circumstances. Let's take a look at the various scenarios you might encounter in trying to determine who's responsible for paying off debt.

Individual Debt

Debts involving just one signature on the dotted line are usually the simplest to figure out. If you sign up for a credit card through a store, for example, and the card is in your name alone, then you can expect to be the only one responsible for making payments.

This scenario holds true for individual loans, too. That means if your child takes out student loans in her name, without a co-signer, she is the only person responsible for making payments In each case of individual debt—whether it's one of the sce-

narios mentioned above, an auto loan or a mortgage—the consequences, whether fines, damage to credit, calls from bill collectors, liens or garnished wages, won't extend to family members as long as the debtor is living. Read on to learn what happens to individual debt when it is passed on to heirs.

Shared Debt

Things get trickier when multiple people are involved, for example if you co-sign a loan.

If you co-sign your child's student loans and she can't make payments, as the co-signer you'll be legally obligated to make them in her place. And if your child misses a payment, your credit score could take a hit—potentially hurting your chances of qualifying for credit in the future.

In the case of credit cards, in most states, you won't be on the hook for your spouse's credit card debt—unless you're a joint account holder. If you *are* a joint account holder, you can be held responsible for payments. If you fail to make payments, the lender can send the account to collections and report you to the credit reporting agencies. However, it's worth noting that being an

> If you co-sign your child's student loans and she can't make payments, as the co-signer you'll be legally obligated to make them in her place.

Know what potential debt you're getting into when you co-sign your child's loans.

authorized user on a card isn't the same as holding the account jointly.

If you and your spouse are both listed on a mortgage, home equity loan or car loan, you're both legally responsible for payments.

In the event of divorce, you and your former spouse will have to divvy up—or continue sharing—the debts that you held jointly. Once you have identified the debts that list both of you as either a borrower or co-signer, you should decide who will take over which loan, and have the other person's name removed.

If your ex-spouse fails to make payments on debts you hold together, your only recourse may be to pursue legal action. If any loan was in your ex-spouse's name alone, however, you have no obligation to make payments—even if you pooled your money and split the bills when you were married.

Inherited Debt

When someone dies, their debts can stubbornly live on. For loved ones dealing with the assets and obligations a relative leaves behind, the situation can be complicated.

PRO TIP

Rules about inherited debt vary from state to state. An estate-planning attorney can help you understand your state's specific rules.

The good news: Unless you were a co-signer, you generally can't be held responsible for paying the debts of any deceased person who wasn't your spouse.

And even in the event of your spouse's death, your responsibility may still be limited under state law.

There are exceptions to that rule:

• If you were a co-signer on a loan
• If you were joint account holders
• If you live in a community property state (Alaska, Arizona, California, Idaho, Louisiana, Nevada, New Mexico, Texas, Washington or Wisconsin), where you may be obligated to use "community property" to pay off your spouse's debts.

> Unless you are co-signing a loan, you can't be held responsible for paying the debts of a deceased person who was not your spouse.

While you typically aren't responsible for paying a loved one's debts, the estate of the deceased may actually be responsible. The assigned executor will handle making debt payments.

In most cases, if an estate doesn't have enough to cover all of the person's debts, those obligations will simply continue to go unpaid. One major exception to this rule that applies in many states: medical bills. If your parent died with outstanding medical bills and the estate can't cover them, adult children can still be held responsible in almost 30 states. Check with your state to see if it applies what are called "filial responsibility" laws.

If you inherit a home or property with a mortgage, you'll eventually be responsible for paying—though not necessarily immediately. If you don't want to take over the mortgage, you can ask the bank for a short sale or tell them to foreclose. An attorney can offer valuable guidance as you decide how to proceed.

When a loved one dies, their debts may be sold to debt collectors who may then contact you, seeking payment. You can refer them to the executor of the estate, but you shouldn't provide any other information over the phone.

Understanding all of the rules around inherited debt can be challenging and confusing. If you need guidance, estate and tax attorneys can help you cut through the complexity, minimize your responsibility and take care of any obligations in the most efficient way possible.

When both spouses are listed on a mortgage, each is responsible for making sure that loan is repaid.

YES, THERE IS SUCH A THING AS "GOOD DEBT"
Debt can be an important part of your financial tool kit

According to the Federal Reserve, in 2019 mortgage balances rose to $9.4 trillion, student loan debt reached $1.5 trillion and auto loans continued their six-year upward trend. Although these numbers may trigger your stress response, having debt can actually be a useful tool—if you manage it correctly. Debt can improve your credit rating, increase your potential for future earnings and allow you to purchase large assets when you can't afford to buy them with cash.

This news isn't an excuse to use your credit card for frivolous spending. Rather, it's an invitation to strategize, set goals and recognize how certain purchases can play a positive role in your overall financial life.

Mortgages are considered "good debt" because real estate values often rise, boosting your net worth.

When Is Debt Useful?

An integral step toward successful debt management is learning which investments can lead to "good debt." Of course, classifying a purchase as good or bad is not a one-size-fits-all equation, as everyone's situation is different. However, simply put: Good debt increases your net worth and creates future value.

Consider mortgages, which are the largest component of national household debt. A mortgage serves several purposes: It allows you to pay off your house at a pace you can afford, provides a structure for budgeting and saving in other areas of your life—such as pumping money into retirement funds—and the house itself hopefully appreciates each year that the market rises. Ideally, when you're ready to move, you can sell the house for more than you originally paid and use the earnings for other goals.

Student loans can also be good debt, based on the premise that borrowing money for a quality education will lead to a well-paying career. This formula is tricky, as not all degrees increase the likelihood of landing a job that justifies the debt. But recent

Before taking out a loan for a new car, consider buying a less-expensive used car that will require less debt.

research from the Bureau of Labor Statistics shows that employees with a bachelor's degree earn over $500 more per week compared to those with a high school diploma and no college experience.

Finally, taking on a variety of debt and making on-time payments can help boost your credit score. Lenders use your credit score—which is calculated based on information from your credit report—to decide whether to give you a loan. In turn, a good credit score can make future lines of credit more accessible and help you land loans with more favorable terms.

Recognizing Bad Debt

Some debt has the potential to increase your net worth and create profitable opportunities for your future. Other debts leave you with assets that don't appreciate in value—and actually lose value over time—or exorbitant interest rates that make it more difficult to pay off. New cars, for example, are much more expensive than their used coun-

terparts, because vehicles begin to lose value the minute they're driven off the lot. Since the return on investment for an automobile is so low—in fact, it's often negative— it can make more sense to buy a less expensive, reliable used car than to go into debt just to get behind the wheel of the latest model.

Credit card debt can also lead you into problematic territory, as interest rates are often high, and the payment schedules are arranged to maximize costs for the consumer. Other options—such as payday loans—let you borrow money to cover short-term expenses, but their very steep interest rates are notorious for trapping consumers in a vicious cycle of debt caused by partial and late payments. Avoid them if you can.

Despite its unpleasant connotations, debt is not always negative. If you can prioritize your financial obligations and pay your bills on time, debt can help you maintain a healthy and fulfilling lifestyle—while building a future for yourself and your family.

YOUR CREDIT REPORT VS. YOUR CREDIT SCORE
Understanding your credit score and credit report can help you land your next loan

To understand the difference between your credit report and your credit score, first imagine taking a test. You fill out the answers to 50 questions. This represents your credit report. When you're finished, your teacher checks your answers and gives you a grade based on the number of questions you got right. That's your credit score.

Each of your debts—such as a mortgage, a car loan or credit card debt—is like an answer on the test. If you've been paying on time and don't have creditors chasing after you, you've filled in the correct answer and your score goes up. But a loan that's in default or a bankruptcy filing is like a wrong answer, and each wrong answer knocks down your credit score. Similarly, having no credit at all (imagine leaving all of the answers blank), can count against you—simply because there's nothing for potential lenders to look at. With this analogy in mind, here's a closer look at credit reports and scores.

The higher your credit score, the more likely lenders are to give you the best deals on loans.

> **PRO TIP**
> The three major credit bureaus offer free access to your credit report once a year. Check each one carefully and report any errors.

Your Credit Report
Your credit report shows your debts, any claims against you, any times you filed for bankruptcy and any credit accounts you have open. In the United States, there are three major credit reporting agencies: Equifax, Experian and TransUnion. Each of these agencies uses similar data to compile reports—but they're not identical. That means some things that show up on your Equifax credit report might not show up on your TransUnion report, and vice versa.

Each item on your credit report will list to whom the debt is owed (your mortgage company, for example), how long the account has been open, the original loan amount (or the credit limit), the remaining balance and your payment history. This in-depth report helps lenders get the full picture of the kind of debt you're already carrying and how you've been managing it.

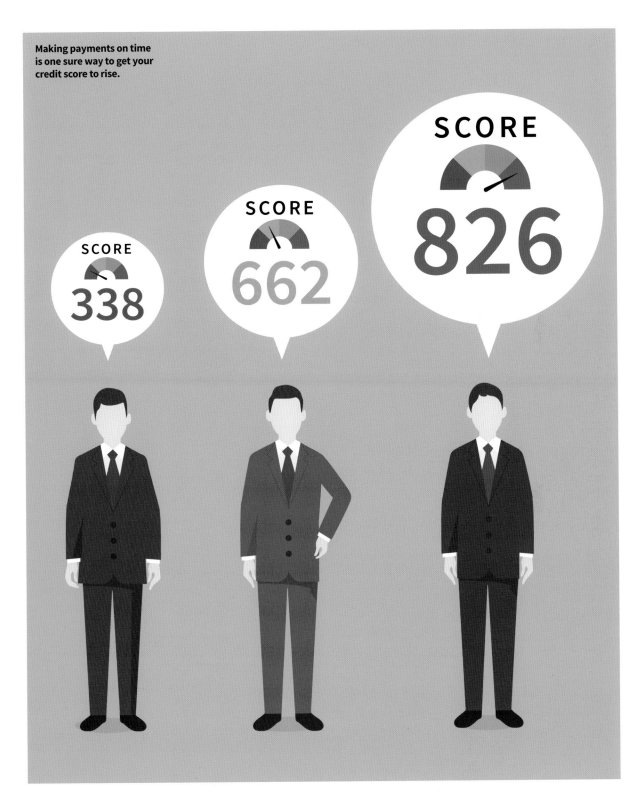

Making payments on time is one sure way to get your credit score to rise.

Although you may be surprised by how thorough your credit report is, it won't contain everything that you might expect. For example, rent payments, utility payments and cellphone payments don't show up on credit reports and won't affect your credit score, either positively or negatively. The exception is when a landlord or utility company sends your debt to a collection agency or files a claim against you. Those events will definitely appear on your credit report.

Other things that don't show up on your credit report are your income, your net worth and how you manage any checking accounts. That's because potential lenders aren't just interested in how much money you make—they're interested in your ability to manage debt and repay it. After all, having plenty of money in the bank doesn't necessarily mean that a person is good at managing that money—or at making payments on time. Likewise, if you're making your scheduled payments every month, even if you don't make a lot of money, lenders will usually see you as a relatively safe bet.

How Your Credit Score Is Calculated

You may have heard your credit score referred to as your FICO score. While TransUnion, Experian and Equifax each compile your credit report, your actual credit score is most often calculated by FICO, an independent company with an algorithm for computing consumer credit-worthiness. Scores will range from 300 to 850, with an average score of around 700. Recently, other companies, such as VantageScore, have begun calculating their own credit scores as well. Though each agency's algorithms may vary, they all generally take five main factors into account when calculating scores:

● **Your Payment History** Lenders want to see that you have a history of making payments on time. This factor has significant weight in the calculation of your credit score. That fact alone should be great motivation to always make loan payments on time.

● **Amount Owed** Maybe you have access to a $10,000 line of credit, but are you actually using it? Lenders are interested in how much debt you already have to date. They're also interested in your credit utilization, or how much of your available credit you're putting to use. Maxing out multiple credit cards can be a red flag to lenders, indicating that you routinely spend more than you have.

● **Length of Credit History** How long you've had your accounts does factor in, which is why it's great to begin establishing credit early. Someone with a long history of making payments will look like less of a risk than someone who suddenly began taking out lines of credit in the past six months.

● **New Credit** Applying for (or opening) multiple accounts can create small dings in your score. It can be an indication that you intend to take on more debt—and may even signal a worsening financial picture. Even if you have one long-term loan that you're paying off (like a 30-year mortgage), a bunch of newer lines of credit will reduce your credit history's average length.

● **Mix of Credit** Is every item on your report a credit card? Lenders like to see how you're able to manage fixed repayments (such as a mortgage that's the same month to month) as well as variable repayments (such as credit cards, which fluctuate month to month).

It's important to keep track of both your credit score and your credit report. Credit reports often contain mistakes that can damage your score if you don't report them. You can get copies of your credit report for free once a year from each of the three credit agencies. Each of these reports can help you understand how you appear to lenders, and what steps you can take to boost your score.

PRO TIP

Lenders like to see a mix of items on your credit report, from revolving debt, such as credit cards, to debts with fixed monthly payments.

Credit Report

Your Credit Score is:

765

250   800

Credit Rating: **EXCELLENT**

Report Summary

Tradeline Overview		Acc
Total:	37	Curr
Current:	32	Acct
Untrade:	0	Acc
Current Neg:	0	Mo
Historical Neg:	1	

Credit reports are not set in stone: You can take steps to improve your score over time.

WHAT HAPPENS WHEN YOU FALL BEHIND?
From default to bankruptcy, here's a look at the consequences of not paying your debt

M issing debt payments or stopping paying your bills altogether can damage your credit score and result in default or collections. As a result, you may find yourself dealing with debt collectors or even considering bankruptcy. Here's a look at what happens when you fall behind on your debt, and strategies for dealing with the consequences.

Default

If you fall behind on your debt payments, your account is considered delinquent. If your account is delinquent for too long, or if you break one of the other terms of your loan agreement, you may be declared in default.

What happens when you default on your debt depends on the type of debt that you have. In the case of a secured debt, which is backed by an asset, such as a mortgage or an auto loan, you ultimately risk losing your house or having your car repossessed. In the case of an unsecured debt, the creditor typically can't claim your property and must attempt to collect on the debt in other ways.

> **PRO TIP**
>
> Specific rules govern how and when debt collectors are allowed to contact you. Make sure you know what's legal—and what's not.

Collections

Once you've defaulted on an unsecured debt, your account may be sent to a collection agency, a third-party firm whose only job is to track you down and get you to pay some or all of what you already owe. Your credit card or loan agreement probably has specific language about when a collection agency will step in. Some agencies buy the debt at a discount from your creditor. Others are hired to collect on your creditor's behalf in exchange for a commission.

Damage to Your Credit Score

When there's no collateral to be seized, most of the leverage debt collectors have over you (besides

When dealing with debt collectors, get everything in writing and keep copies of all communications.

A debt collector may remove the collection account from your credit report in exchange for full payment.

their persistence) is your credit score. If your credit score hasn't already suffered from the missed payments, it will once the collection agency gets involved. A collection account is one of the most damaging items on a credit report, and it can affect your score even after you've paid it off, for up to seven years.

How to Deal With Debt Collectors

Debt collectors have very specific rules they must follow. They can't call you before 8 a.m. or after 9 p.m., and they can't call you at work once you tell them not to. While they are allowed to call your neighbors or family members to verify your contact information, they aren't allowed to tell them any details about your debt. If you send the collection agency a written cease-and-desist letter, they're bound by federal law to stop contacting you about the debt. In this case, you can expect a final letter from the agency outlining what actions they plan to take to collect the debt.

If the debt is old enough, you may be protected by a statute of limitations, which varies from state to state. But while you attempt to wait it out, your credit score will tank. In the meantime, your creditor may turn to the courts to put a lien on your property, seize your assets or start pulling money out of your paycheck.

The first thing you can do when a debt collector calls is to ask for the information in writing. If you are going to dispute the debt, you need to send a letter by certified mail, so that you can be sure the debt collector received it.

If you can't dispute the debt, you can still try to negotiate it down. Some debt collectors will accept a fraction of your debt obligation just to settle the issue. You could also offer to pay the amount in full in exchange for the debt collector removing the collection account from your credit report. If you

> If you can't dispute the debt, try negotiating. Some debt collectors will accept a smaller payment just to settle the issue.

can come to an agreement, wait to pay until you get the deal in writing.

Whatever your approach is, keep track of all written communications and phone calls with the collection agency, saving voice mails, emails and letters. To protect yourself, keep your conversations short, and never give debt collectors your bank account information.

You no longer have the legal obligation to pay a debt that's discharged in a bankruptcy filing. Collection agencies should stop calling you about them, and they can't sue you or garnish your wages over them.

Unfortunately, filing for bankruptcy won't remove a lien on your assets, and some types of debt simply can't be erased. They include child support, alimony, most student loans and most unpaid taxes.

If you forget to list a dischargeable debt in your bankruptcy filing, the debt is not discharged. That means even after you file for bankruptcy, creditors that didn't participate in the bankruptcy process may still be able to collect on debts.

Credit Cards

The dos and don'ts of paying with plastic

CREDIT CARD BASICS If you want to make the most of credit cards, first you need to know how they work

Ah, credit cards. These ubiquitous pieces of plastic can be great financial tools, but they can also lead you down a path of ever-increasing debt. Before you start using credit cards—or even if you've already got a wallet full of them—make sure you know the basics of how they work.

Applying for a Card

Just because you *want* a credit card doesn't mean you'll qualify for one. Like any lenders, credit card companies want to make sure you have the resources and discipline to pay back your debts. When you apply for a credit card, the issuer will look at your credit score, your income and any other debts you already have. If they like what they see, they'll offer you a card with specific terms and a set credit limit.

Credit Limits

Your credit limit is a cap on the amount of money that the issuer is willing to lend you at a given time. When people say they've "maxed out" their credit cards, they mean that they've reached their credit limit. If your credit limit is $1,000 and you charge $1,000 in goods and services to your card, you've reached your credit limit and can't make any more charges until you pay off some or all of your balance. Make a $150 payment and you'll have $150 in available credit again.

If you do max out your credit cards, or anticipate a large expense, you can ask your card's issuer to raise your credit limit. It's a good idea to limit this option to emergencies when you need to cover unexpected expenses. Whether your issuer will raise your limit or not depends on how reliably you've been making your payments and how much of your credit you're already using. Aim to keep your spending well below your credit limit. In fact, using more than 30% of your limit can negatively affect your credit score.

Making Your Monthly Payment

Unlike installment loans, such as mortgages, credit cards operate on revolving debt. That's because

Credit cards are great for paying big expenses over time, but interest costs can start to add up.

49

Consider moving debt from high-interest cards to lower-interest ones to save money.

the amount you owe changes month to month and day to day. Your debt grows when you spend and shrinks when you make a payment. Each month, you'll receive a bill from your card's issuer, listing your monthly activity and your total balance. You aren't required to pay the whole balance immediately, though you should, whenever possible. Your card company will list a minimum payment you must make, which is generally around 2% of what you owe. If that amount is too small, the minimum payment may be a flat amount—perhaps around $25.

Whatever you don't pay remains on your balance and accrues interest until you pay it off. That means you'll actually owe more next month than you do right now, even if you don't make any new purchases. In short, the smaller your payments, the more you'll end up paying over time.

Interest and APR

The amount of interest you pay each month is determined by your APR (annual percentage rate)

> Like any lenders, credit card companies want to make sure you have the resources and discipline to pay your debts.

and your average daily balance. Credit card companies calculate interest daily, so the lower your average daily balance, the less interest you'll accrue. For example, if you've carried over a $1,000 balance from last month, but you plan to pay off $700 of it this month, make that payment as early in the billing cycle as possible. By knocking off $700 early in the month, you'll significantly lower your daily balance for the rest of the month and pay much less in interest.

The Grace Period

Just because you use your credit card doesn't mean you'll necessarily pay interest. Credit cards also have something called a grace period, during which you don't accrue any interest on your debt. The grace period is the time between the end of your billing cycle and when your payment is due. If you can pay off your balance in full before the due date, you won't pay any interest at all. This is the best way to use your credit card; it keeps your credit in good shape and ensures that you'll make the most of any rewards that your card offers.

WHAT TYPES OF CREDIT CARDS ARE OUT THERE?

You'll want to check out the different types of credit cards available before you decide to apply. Pay attention to the details: Cards that offer big perks may also come with high interest rates. Here's a look:

Store Cards Many retailers offer credit cards that can only be used in their own stores. They're essentially a loyalty program, offering rewards for your business.

Branded Store Cards Other retailers offer cards that are co-branded with a company like Visa or Mastercard. You can use these cards anywhere you would a normal credit card, while potentially earning rewards with that retailer.

Cash-Back Cards Many cards offer "cash-back" rewards, giving you back a percentage of what you've spent.

Bank-Issued Cards Besides a regular credit card, your bank may offer a secured credit card if your credit isn't great, or a line of credit that you can attach to your checking account in case of overdrafts.

Travel-Reward Cards Many airlines offer cards that give you "miles" for every dollar you spend. You can trade them in for free flights, upgrades and other travel benefits.

CREDIT CARD MISTAKES TO AVOID Don't let convenience become an excuse for letting your guard down

Let's face it, credit cards are a very convenient—but sometimes tricky—financial tool. They make it unnecessary to carry around large amounts of cash, and they can help bridge the financial gap between today and the next payday. But all that convenience can come at a high price—including fines, interest payments and damage to your credit rating. Fortunately, these outcomes aren't a given if you're careful. Start by avoiding these common credit card mistakes.

If you're not careful, credit cards can go from a convenient tool to a major financial burden.

Spending Money You Don't Have

Your credit card gives you a large amount of spending power, but that doesn't mean you have to use it. Remember that you still have to pay your card off at some point—and the longer you wait to pay it off, the more it will cost you in the long run. You'll pay for the convenience of a card due to the high interest card companies charge when you carry a balance.

> **PRO TIP**
> Making minimum payments on your card gives you more time to pay off your balance, but will also cost you more in interest.

Once you outstrip your ability to make a card payment, you open yourself up to other mistakes that compound your costs. For example, making only minimum payments on your card extends the amount of time it takes to pay back your debt—but it also maximizes the amount of interest you'll pay on outstanding balances over that time. Paying your card in full every month is ideal, but short of that, it's usually best to pay as much as you possibly can.

Hurting Your Credit

If you can't even make the minimum payment on your credit card balance, you may find yourself making late payments or, worse, missing payments entirely. When you miss payments, you expose yourself to late fees. Card companies can also penalize you for late payments by charging higher interest rates on your outstanding balance than they normally do.

Credit cards give you plenty of spending power, but don't be tempted to spend more money than you can repay.

53

Miss enough payments and you could be in for what card companies call a "charge-off." That's when you get far enough behind on payments that the card company declares your debt a loss. A charge-off can affect your credit rating for up to seven years, making it significantly more difficult to get credit cards or other types of loans. It's best to avoid that situation at all costs.

Other Credit-Related Mistakes

Late or missing payments may be the easiest way to tank your credit score, but there are also several less-obvious ways to ding your credit. For example, part of your credit score is based on how much of a balance you carry compared to the amount of overall credit you have. The closer your balance gets to your credit limit, the worse your score gets, so maxing out your cards can create problems. It may not be obvious, but closing unused credit cards can cause your credit score to drop as well. That's because doing so drops your overall credit limit closer to your current balances—the same effect as maxing out your cards.

Not Paying Attention

Your credit card agreement and your monthly statement may not make for exciting reading, but that doesn't mean it's OK to ignore them. There's a lot of important information buried in the fine print. For example, knowing your card's terms can help you avoid unnecessary fees, such as those charged for cash advances. Some cards charge fees for foreign transactions, while others don't. Knowing which is which can save you money on an overseas vacation.

It's even more important to read your monthly statement carefully. Credit cards offer protection from fraudulent charges, but only if you notice them and dispute them in a timely manner. Reading your statement will also ensure you make your payments on time and stay up to date on any changes to your terms—all of which can keep you from making bigger, more costly mistakes.

PRO TIP

Credit card agreements may not be exciting, but paying attention to the fine print can help you avoid pesky fees and penalties.

Before making that knock-out purchase, create a self-imposed spending limit on your credit cards.

HOW TO CHOOSE THE RIGHT CREDIT CARD
The first step in selecting a credit card is determining how you'll use it

You've decided to get a new credit card? Great! But before you start filling out the application, ask yourself how you plan to use your new card. Will it only be for emergencies? Or are you anticipating using it immediately for a large expense, such as a vacation? Are you trying to build or repair your credit? Or do you hope to rack up points with your favorite airline or hotel chain? Knowing the answer will help you narrow down your options and choose a card that works for you.

You Need to Build Credit

Much like the old saying, "it takes money to make money," it usually takes credit to get credit. Credit card companies want to see that you know how to manage debt before they take a risk on you. Luckily, secured credit cards can get you started. You'll often qualify for one even with poor or no credit. Secured credit cards function like regular credit cards, but require a cash deposit on your end—often around $200. The deposit secures the debt in the event that you can't make your payments. When you eventually close the account in good standing, or are upgraded to a regular credit card,

> Credit card companies want to see that you know how to manage debt before they take a risk on you. Luckily, secured credit cards can get you started. You'll often qualify for one even with poor or no credit.

you'll get your deposit back. Secured credit cards are a great way to improve or build your credit, which can help you get approved for other types of cards in the future.

It's Only for Emergencies

A credit card can be a lifesaver when you need to cover an unexpected expense. If you only plan to use your card for emergencies, look for a card with no annual fee and a low interest rate. You want something that doesn't cost you anything if you don't use it, and that will cost you as little as possible when you do. Don't be seduced by promises of zero interest for the first year, since you may not even use it until that introductory rate has expired.

You've Got a Big Expense Coming Up

If you have a large expense that you plan to charge, look for a card that offers a long introductory period with no interest. Many companies offer zero-interest rates for the first six to 18 months. That means you won't pay any interest for that period, and your entire payment each month will go toward paying down your balance. Create a budget

Getting receipts whenever you make purchases helps remind you that you are incurring debt.

and plan to make the largest payments you can afford to during the introductory period. That way, you get the most out of the zero-interest period. If you can pay off the entire balance before the introductory period ends, congratulations—you just got an interest-free loan.

You're Looking to Cash In on Rewards

PRO TIP

Do the math: If the rewards you earn don't add up to more than the annual fees for a card, you're losing money.

Credit card companies love to entice consumers with promises of cash back, airline miles and insider deals at retail stores. Some of these rewards can add up to significant perks. However, miles and points can expire when you're not looking, or be subject to restrictions that make them less than ideal. Make sure to read—and understand—the fine print before you sign on the dotted line.

IS A REWARDS CARD RIGHT FOR YOU?

Rewards are a huge draw for consumers. They can help you save money that you would have spent anyway. Or you can earn points or miles that can help you buy that new smartphone or that trip to Costa Rica.

But if you don't pay your balance every month, they aren't as good a deal. Every month you carry a balance, you accrue interest. And most of the time, that interest costs more than the value of your rewards you've picked up in the meantime. If your credit card company gives you 2% cash back, but you're paying 18% interest, who's really getting the better deal?

Don't be afraid
to ask your card
issuer for lower
interest rates or
other bonus perks.

GET THE MOST OUT OF YOUR CREDIT CARD
A little knowledge can help you stay in control

Most Americans carry a credit card balance from month to month, and it can be increasingly difficult to get out of debt if it continues piling up. However, there are things you can do to make it easier to pay off your bill and save money along the way.

Balance Transfers

If you're struggling to pay off your high-interest credit card debt, a balance transfer can be a lifeline. With a balance transfer, you move your debt from one credit card (generally one with a high interest rate) to a new credit card (often one with a lower APR). You may even be able to find a card that offers a 12- or 18-month introductory period with no interest. During that time, pay off as much of your balance as you can in order to get the full benefit of the transfer. But be aware that when the introductory period is over, interest rates may skyrocket—perhaps even higher than your previous rate.

If your card issuer allows balance transfers, you can expect to pay between 3% and 5% of the total amount you transfer. Even with this fee, a balance transfer can help put more money toward paying down your debt and less toward paying interest.

Request a Lower Rate

Sure, the last mailing you received from your credit card company said your rate is currently 21%, but does it have to be? It doesn't hurt to call them up and ask.

Credit card companies rely on the fact that many people simply pay the monthly minimum and leave it at that. However, if you're willing to call up your credit card company and request a lower interest rate—perhaps noting that yours is above the national average, or that you've received better offers from other companies—they may offer to lower it.

Automate Your Payments

Automating payments prevents you from missing a payment or triggering late fees, saving you money and protecting your credit score. Credit card companies will often offer automated payments that only cover the monthly minimum—so you'll end up paying maximum interest over time. And because automation makes it easier to forget about your credit card bill, it can also make it easier to overspend and rack up more debt. To avoid this, consider how much you can realistically afford to pay each month and set the withdrawal to that amount.

Use Your Card Everywhere

Rewards can add up fast—just be careful not to overdo it. If you can keep your spending in check and you've budgeted to be able to pay your entire balance at the end of each month, putting everything on your card is a great way to maximize any rewards your card offers.

PRO TIP

Some balance transfer offers include an introductory period with 0% interest. That can help if you're trying to pay off a big balance.

Real Estate

The ins and outs of the "good debt" you
can accrue to buy or renovate a home

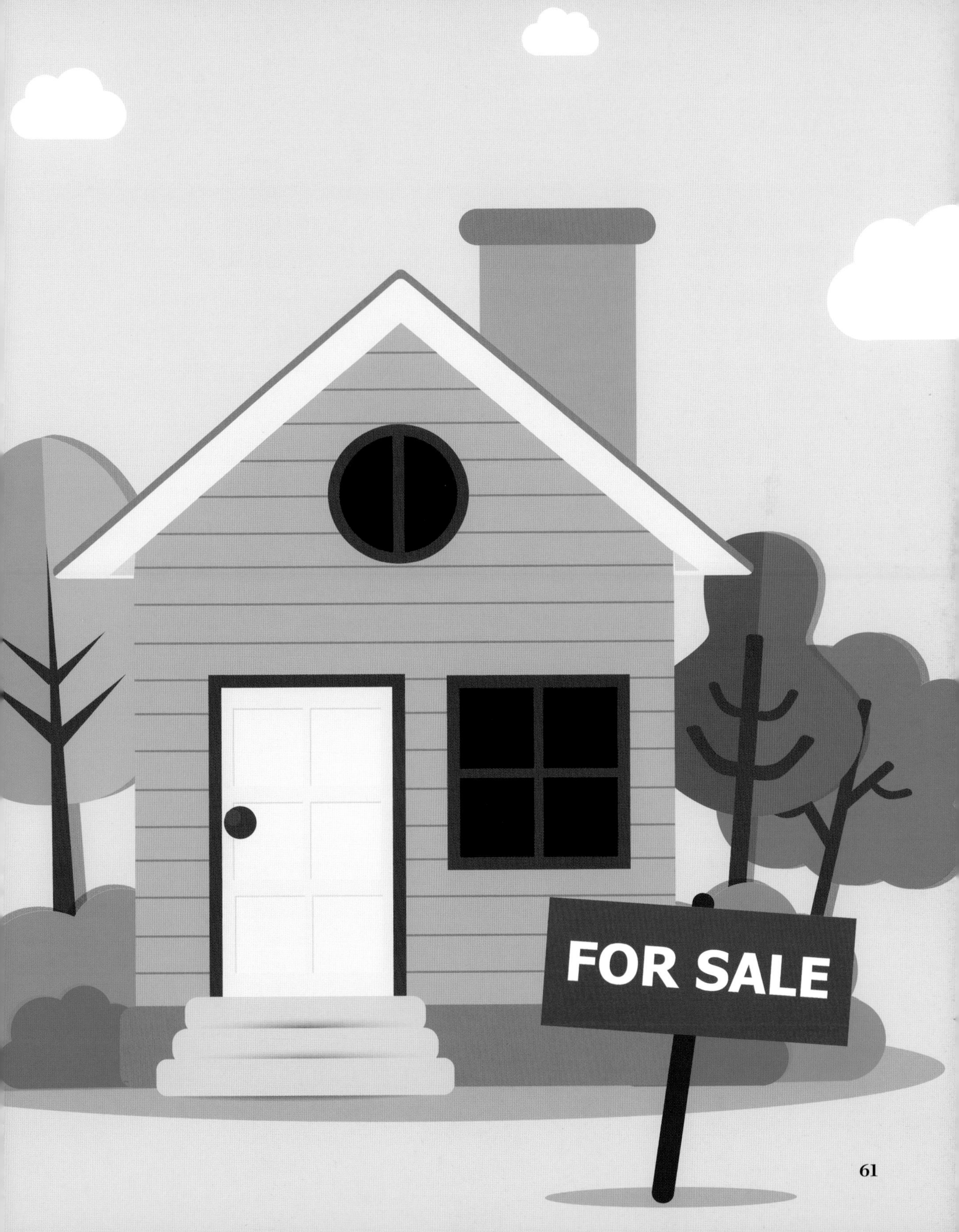
FOR SALE

MORTGAGE BASICS When you want to buy a house, a condominium or a plot of land, there's a good chance you won't be able to pay for it from your checking account. Like most homebuyers, you'll likely need a mortgage

So, what is a mortgage? In simple terms, it's a loan to buy real estate. The money comes from a bank, and then the bank actually owns your home. When you sign a mortgage, you promise to pay back the loan (with interest) in monthly installments. But promises get broken sometimes, so the bank protects its investment by keeping the deed to your home. If you don't pay, they can sell your house to recoup their money.

Of course, the bank doesn't really want to own your home. Ideally, you'll make your payments on time, and cut the grass. In other words, you and the bank want the same thing: you, living in your dream home and making payments you can afford. Here's a look at how it can happen.

The Two Basic Types of Mortgages

Mortgages come in all different types, and banks keep inventing new flavors, but basically you have two choices: fixed rate and adjustable rate.

● **Fixed Rate** Most mortgages are fixed-rate: The interest rate is set at the beginning, and it never changes for the life of the mortgage. A fixed-rate mortgage could be bad news if rates fall over time. But when rates tumble, homeowners often turn to refinancing—essentially replacing their current mortgage with a new mortgage that has a lower interest rate.

● **Adjustable Rate** With an adjustable-rate mortgage, also known as an ARM, your rate usually starts low—often way below market rates. This introductory rate is called a teaser rate, and with good reason: It doesn't last. After a set period—perhaps five years—the rate will "reset," which could mean your monthly payment will skyrocket. After the reset, the rate on your loan will go up or down more gradually, often annually.

The low teaser rate means you can afford to buy a more expensive home. The danger is that the reset rate can cause budget shock. For that reason, ARMs are best if you're not planning to own a home for a long time, or if you believe your income will increase significantly before the reset.

FHA and VA Mortgages

Low-income buyers may be eligible for mortgages underwritten by the Federal Housing Administration. They feature low interest rates, and down payments as low as 3.5% of the purchase price. Veterans and active-duty service members may qualify

Factor in all of the costs of owning a house beyond the initial purchase price, from necessary renovations to upkeep.

for mortgages from the Department of Veterans Affairs. These VA loans also have low rates, and may even let buyers purchase a home with no down payment.

The Down Payment

With few exceptions (like a VA loan) you'll need to come up with some of the purchase price yourself; banks don't like loaning money to people who have no skin in the game.

Traditionally, banks require a 20% down payment, but you can often get away with less by paying private mortgage insurance (PMI). This premium gets

Traditionally, banks require a 20 percent down payment, but you can often get away with less by paying what's known as private mortgage insurance (PMI).

rolled into your monthly payment, and covers the bank if you skip out .

Making a larger down payment also means your mortgage lender may give you a lower interest rate. And the more you pay up front, the less you'll pay in interest over the life of the mortgage.

About That Interest Rate...

Interest rates are sneaky things. The difference between 4.0% and 4.5% might seem small. But let's say you're taking out a 30-year fixed-rate mortgage to buy a $300,000 house, and making a down payment of 20%. A mortgage with an interest rate of 4% will cost you a total of roughly $515,000 over the life of the loan. But at 4.5%, you'll pay around $540,000—an increase of about $25,000. With that kind of money at stake, it pays to shop for the best rate.

Mortgage rates can rise and fall due to several factors, including the economy, inflation and even the health of the housing market. But the rate you actually get quoted will depend on your personal financial situation—meaning your credit score, income, existing debt, the size of your down payment and even the size of your overall loan.

The bank will consider your finances and hopefully give you what's called pre-qualification for a loan amount and interest rate. This is no guarantee, but it means you're in the ballpark, so you can start shopping for a home.

Closing Costs

Closing costs are the fees you pay at the mortgage signing, typically 2% to 5% of the loan amount. You can often roll closing costs into the loan, which means you'll be paying them for years to come, with interest.

Some closing costs cover outside services—such as an appraiser to verify the property's value, or a title search to guarantee there are no liens on the deed. And you will probably need to pay homeowner's insurance and property taxes up-front. Once you get approved for a mortgage on an actual home, the bank will give you a loan estimate, which spells out the closing costs.

PRO TIP

Getting a mortgage involves lots—and lots—of paperwork. Be sure to read the fine print so you know exactly what you're signing up for.

Closing day can be nerve-racking. But once you sign all that paperwork, you'll get the keys to your new castle. If you've done your homework, you'll cross the threshold with a fair interest rate, a monthly payment you can afford—and some money left over to buy curtains.

Veterans and active-duty service members may qualify for low-cost mortgages.

HOW MUCH MORTGAGE CAN YOU AFFORD?
Know what you can spend for your dream home

Shopping for a new home is exciting and, at times, overwhelming. The big question: What kind of house can you afford? After all, nothing kills the joy of owning a home quicker than drowning in loan payments trying to hold on to it. Here's a look at how to determine how much house you can afford.

Consider Your Income

One rule of thumb says housing costs shouldn't exceed 28% of gross income (the money you make before taxes are taken out). Start by calculating your pre-tax income, including your salary and any other cash that you have coming in. If your family's annual income is $72,000, or $6,000 a month, you could afford housing costs of up to $1,680 a month.

However, "housing costs" include homeowner's insurance and property taxes, among other expenses. You'll need to pay these on top of your loan amount. When calculating monthly housing costs, factor in these expenses.

Banks often look at that 28% calculation when deciding your mortgage total. But just because a bank will loan you that amount doesn't mean you should accept it. Look at your budget and other financial goals to figure out a comfortable monthly payment.

> **PRO TIP**
> **Your credit score and the size of your down payment, along with interest rates, are the major factors that affect mortgage costs.**

Factor in Your Down Payment

How much money you're able to put down when you buy has a big impact on your mortgage payment. If you've saved a large amount, say 20% or more, your mortgage costs will be much less than if you make a down payment of 10%. And if your down payment is less than 20%, you'll need to pay—and budget for—private mortgage insurance (PMI).

Identify the Wiggle Room

Interest payments are a big part of your monthly mortgage expenses, and if you can reduce them, you'll be able to afford more house with the money available to you each month.

When setting your interest rate, banks will consider your debt-to-income ratio (DTI)—that is, your total debt as a percentage of your pre-tax income. Most banks want to see a DTI below 35%. That means the total of your monthly student loans, car loans, credit card payments and the mortgage you're applying for can't exceed 35% of your salary. Reducing your DTI by paying off debts can lead banks to offer more favorable interest rates.

Conventional mortgages typically require a credit score of 620 or above; you can qualify for an FHA loan with a score as low as 580. Raising your score by paying off debt can also lead to more favorable interest rates.

Just because a bank offers a
big mortgage doesn't mean it's
right for your budget.

MORTGAGE MISTAKES
Eight mortgage missteps you'll want to avoid

Mistakes happen, but unfortunately, mortgage mistakes can haunt you for decades. Here's a list of pitfalls that can cost you big if you don't avoid them.

Mortgage mess-ups can be expensive—and it's easier to avoid them than to fix them.

• **You Didn't Shop Around** According to the National Consumer Protection Bureau (NCPB), almost half of all borrowers simply apply for the very first mortgage that they find—without shopping around for rates online, or even locally. Bad move: The NCPB points out what a difference just half a percentage point makes. Say you're signing a 30-year fixed-rate loan for $200,000. The difference between getting a rate of 4% and 4.5% equals $60 a month—or nearly $22,000 over the life of the loan.

• **You Joined the ARMs Race** Adjustable-rate mortgages (ARMs) come with a low teaser rate that sucks in a lot of buyers. That rate can double or triple after the introductory period ends, typically one to five years later. ARMs can make sense if you're planning to move before the interest rate resets. But for most people, it's a dangerous gamble that can leave you financially stretched—or even unable to make your payments.

• **You Discounted the Down Payment** Some lenders will write you a mortgage with little or even no down payment, but you will pay for their benevolence in much higher interest rates, not to mention costly private mortgage insurance (PMI). That insurance could easily add $100 or more to your monthly payment—and you'll be paying it for years. (FHA loans require PMI for the life of the mortgage). Your best bet is to save up a 20% down payment—and pay less later.

• **You Borrowed Too Much** Banks are often happy to loan you more than you can afford. But it's *your* job, not theirs, to look out for your own budget. Buying a house you can't afford, commonly known as being "house poor," is a terrible feeling. What good is a grand home if you can't afford to buy furniture? Buy a home you can afford, and as your income and family grow, you can always sell it, then upgrade.

Thinking about a fixer upper? Calculate those added expenses in advance.

• **You Ignored the APR** Lenders tease buyers with rock-bottom interest rates, but often those rates are a mirage. They might not include high closing costs, or "points," which are percentages of the loan you must pay up-front to get that brilliant deal. The true cost is reflected in the annual percentage rate (APR), which by law must include all those factors. Be sure to compare APRs, not apples and oranges.

• **You Didn't Negotiate the Fees** Banks can make a lot of money on closing costs. Yet, some of those costs—such as origination fees, document charges, courier services—are negotiable. Don't be afraid to ask which ones are, and ask to have them lowered or waived.

• **You Failed to Factor In Home Expenses** Many first-time buyers are surprised by what it costs to keep up a home. Home expenses can be tough to predict, but one rule of thumb is to budget 1 to 2% of a home's value every year on maintenance and repairs. Make sure your mortgage payment leaves room for those bills.

• **You Failed to Get Pre-Approval** It's easy to get pre-qualified for a mortgage, which means a bank is taking your word on your income and debt, then giving you a ballpark loan amount. A bit more involved, but much better, is pre-approval, which entails actually applying for a loan.

PRO TIP

Shopping around for the best interest rate on a mortgage is unlikely to hurt your credit score (making other requests for credit can).

Why is that better? Because pre-approval requires documentation of your finances and a credit check. That lets the bank give you a conditional commitment for a specific loan amount. When you're negotiating to buy a home, a pre-approval letter is a bargaining chip, since sellers want to avoid potential buyers whose financing might fall through.

Don't forget to shop
around for an interest rate.
It can save you thousands
over the life of the loan.

HOW HELOCS CAN HELP—AND SOMETIMES HURT

A home equity line of credit can be a flexible source of cash when you need it, but it has its own drawbacks

As you pay down your mortgage and the value of your home rises over time, you're building up equity. One of the ways you can tap the value of your home is to take out a home equity line of credit, or HELOC. This can be a convenient way to access cash quickly, but it's worth considering the risks as you weigh your options.

HELOC Basics

A HELOC is a revolving credit line that uses your home as collateral and functions a lot like a credit card. When you take out a HELOC, you get a line of credit that's available to you during a set period—such as 10 years—known as the draw period. You can then draw on those funds with checks or a card whenever you need to, and you'll only pay interest on the amount you use.

PRO TIP

Your credit score plays a big role as a lender makes a decision whether to offer you a HELOC, and at what terms and interest rate.

To determine the amount of your credit line, a lender will consider an appraisal of your home and your ability to make payments. Typically they'll look at your em-

ployment status, sources of income, credit history and other debts you have. A HELOC offers either an interest-only draw period or a draw period that allows you to pay both interest and principal at once.

When to Use a HELOC

HELOCs can make sense in situations where you don't need a large lump sum immediately. For example, they can come in handy if you need to pay for an ongoing home renovation project, like a kitchen or bathroom upgrade.

The Tax Cuts and Jobs Act of 2017 amended the tax code to allow homeowners to deduct the inter-

Take time to map out how
your home equity loan will
impact your finances.

A HELOC can provide the cash you need for home renovation projects.

est on mortgages or home equity debt you use to "substantially improve" your home. The IRS now allows a married couple to deduct the interest on up to $750,000 of eligible debt. That rule means you could actually be increasing the equity in your home while getting a tax break from the government.

You may also consider using a HELOC to pay off other high-interest debt, such as credit card debt. Say your HELOC has an interest rate of 5% while you have credit card debt with a 13% interest rate. Paying off the credit card can help you save more money in the long run, since it's relatively cheaper to pay back the interest on your HELOC.

HELOC Pitfalls

The interest rate on HELOCs is tied to a benchmark interest rate, such as the U.S. Prime Rate. Unless your lender allows you to convert to a fixed rate, a HELOC will likely have a variable interest rate that moves up or down according to the benchmark rate. So it's not uncommon to experience rate increases.

Another risk of borrowing against equity is that a stumbling real estate market could leave you owing more than your home is worth. This scenario is exactly what many homeowners faced when the housing market crashed.

Using your home as collateral also means that you're reducing your home equity, which in turn means you'll make less on the sale of your home when you eventually decide to sell it.

The biggest risk with a HELOC is the potential of foreclosure if you fall behind on your payments. If you go through a tough patch that keeps you from making payments, the consequences could be quite severe.

HELOCs can give you a lot of financial flexibility, letting you tap into a designated line of credit only when you need it. As long as you understand how these loans work and are aware of the potential risks, a HELOC can be a handy tool in your financial tool box.

MORTGAGE REFINANCING
A look at the benefits and risks associated with refinancing your home loan

If you own your home, it's likely your biggest asset—and your mortgage may be your biggest debt. So it's worth considering how well your mortgage is working for you. Mortgage refinancing allows you to replace your old mortgage with a new, possibly better loan. While refinancing can save you money, it can also be an expensive process. Before deciding to refinance, here are some of the factors to consider.

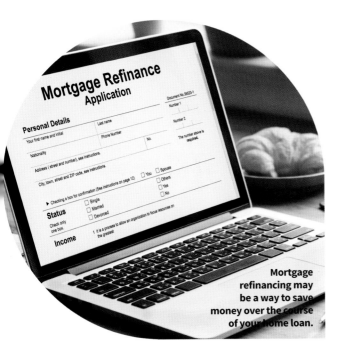

Mortgage refinancing may be a way to save money over the course of your home loan.

The Benefits of Refinancing

When you refinance your mortgage, you are essentially taking out a new loan that pays off your original mortgage. The goal typically is to get a new loan with a more favorable interest rate or a term that works better for you.

A lower interest rate can help you reduce your monthly payment and save money over the life of the loan. You may also be able to adjust the length of the mortgage, shortening it to pay off your loan faster. Or you may be able to lengthen your term, which will reduce the size of your monthly payments and free up money for other financial goals.

If you have a variable-rate mortgage, such as an adjustable rate mortgage, you can refinance into a mortgage with a fixed-rate. Doing so will keep your monthly payments more stable, which in turn may help you more easily manage your household finances.

You can use any money you save through a refinance to help pay down your mortgage faster. Or you may want to consider directing the extra cash toward paying down higher-interest debt. For example, if you carry a high credit card balance with a 14% APR, you may save more money in the long term by paying off that debt than by making extra payments on a mortgage that carries a 4% interest rate.

When You Should Refinance

Consider refinancing your mortgage when interest rates are low. Keep an eye on the Federal Reserve. When it lowers the federal funds rate, mortgage lenders may lower their rates in turn. When the Fed raises rates, it becomes more expensive for banks to borrow from each other, and that cost often is passed on to consumers through higher interest rates.

Likewise, if your credit score has improved since you got a mortgage, a refinance may be worth looking into. Banks look at your score to determine how risky it may be to loan you money. The higher your score is, the more likely they are to offer you a favorable loan with lower interest rates and favorable terms.

> Mortgage rates can fluctuate daily, so track them if you are considering refinancing yours.

The Risks

Unfortunately, refinancing isn't free. Origination fees, appraisal fees, title insurance and other costs can add up quickly. A refi doesn't really start to benefit you until it has offset these costs—and it may never pay for itself. Carefully calculate how long it will take you to break even when determining whether to refinance. (Use an online refinancing calculator to run the numbers.)

Also, ask your current mortgage lender if refinancing will trigger a prepayment fee. If that fee is large enough to cancel the benefits of a refinance, you may be better off sticking to your original mortgage.

Finally, know that lengthening your term may mean paying more in interest over the life of the loan. This isn't necessarily bad, especially if you're using the money you save to tackle higher-interest debt. But do your homework before you refinance to make sure it makes sense in the long run.

It's important to run the numbers to make sure a mortgage refinance makes sense.

A PULLOUT GUIDE TO MORTGAGES Your handy introduction to the wide world of home loans

When shopping around for a mortgage, you'll find plenty of options—and more than a little legal and financial jargon, which can often leave you scratching your head. This quick-and-easy guide to mortgages can help you decipher and understand these complex borrowing tools so you can make an informed choice.

Term Lengths

A mortgage's term length describes how long it will take to pay off.

30-Year This is the most common term length for a mortgage, and it can also be the easiest to qualify for (depending on your age). Because repayment is spread out over a long term, the monthly payments tend to be lower than they are with shorter term mortgages.

> **PRO TIP**
> If you're financially able, making additional payments on your mortgage's principal can help shorten the length of the loan.

15-Year This much shorter term mortgage usually comes with a lower interest rate than a longer mortgage. It's popular with those who can afford to pay more each month but want to save on interest over the length of the loan.

- While 30- and 15-year mortgages are the most popular, mortgage terms can actually range from five to 40 years.

Fixed vs. Adjustable Interest Rates

All mortgages have an interest rate, which will determine how much you pay each month.

Fixed Rate A fixed-rate mortgage maintains the same interest rate for the length of the loan. That means your principal and interest payments never change, even over a 30-year mortgage.

- If interest rates drop during the term of your mortgage, you may be able to refinance in order to benefit from new, lower rates.

Adjustable-Rate An adjustable-rate mortgage (ARM) has an interest rate that changes periodically. The initial interest rate is usually lower than the going fixed rate for mortgages, which can make them tempting if you want to keep monthly payments low. But that rate is almost certain to go up over time.

- There are limits to how often—and by how much—your interest rate can fluctuate, and the rate is generally tied to a specific index, such as the LIBOR index or the U.S. Prime Rate.

- ARMs generally have numbers associated with them that describe when the interest rate can change. For example:

  5-1 ARM For the first five years, the interest rate will stay the same, then it will change each year for the duration of the loan.

3-27 ARM For the first three years, the interest rate on this 30-year loan will stay the same, but will then change annually for the next 27 years.

If you're unclear what a mortgage's number means, ask the lender to explain it to you.

Other Types of Mortgages

Interest-Only Mortgage This type of mortgage gives you the option to make payments only on the loan's interest for a set amount of time (often five to 10 years). Your monthly payments will be lower during this time, but you won't be building any equity since you aren't paying down the loan's principal.

Jumbo Mortgage A jumbo mortgage is a loan beyond what the federal government is able to guarantee. In most of the U.S., the mortgage cap for a single-family home is $510,400. Mortgages above that amount will require a jumbo loan. Typically, to qualify for a jumbo loan, you'll need great credit, and significant assets, along with a large down payment.

Balloon Mortgage Balloon mortgages tend to be shorter-term, usually five or seven years. But despite the short length, the loan is amortized like a 30-year loan. In other words, you'll make small payments for the length of the loan, leaving most of the balance to be paid in one lump sum when the loan ends. Generally, these kinds of mortgages work for people expecting a large windfall that they can use for that final "balloon" payment.

Special Mortgage Programs

Federal Housing Administration Loans These mortgages are backed by the federal government and are intended to make buying a home easier for first-time buyers and those with low to moderate incomes. In many cases, your down payment can be as little as 3.5% of the loan.

Veterans Affairs Backed by the U.S. Department of Veterans Affairs, these loans are available only to U.S. military servicemembers and veterans. They do not require a down payment or mortgage insurance, but there is a VA funding fee that can be as high as 2.3% for first-time users.

USDA If you're looking to buy in a rural area, the United States Department of Agriculture may be able to fund a loan for you. These loans don't require a down payment but there are restrictions regarding what your income must be relative to your monthly payments.

79

Student Loans

The financial impact of getting a diploma can last well beyond college graduation

STUDENT LOAN BASICS
Student debt comes in many different forms, with varying rules on repayment

As tuition costs rise, most Americans use student loans as a tool to open the doors to higher education. In 2019, more than two-thirds of college students took out loans. They're part of the nearly 25% of Americans who are paying off student loans—and if you add those loans together, their student debt load totals about $1.6 trillion.

Student loans can play an important role in helping you accomplish your goals and reach your career ambitions. But taking on loans that you might be paying off for 10, 20 or even 30 years warrants serious consideration. If you're thinking about applying for education loans, or you're figuring out the alternatives available for paying for your child's college education, it's useful to know your student loan basics.

Ways to Use Student Loans

Student loans are unlike other forms of debt because they're specifically intended to fund higher education. They're typically easier to get than other types of loans, and they often offer lower interest rates. And while student loans can—and should—be used to help pay for college tuition and fees, they can also help offset living expenses. That means you can use them for books and school supplies, plus lots of other necessities related to campus living. Groceries, transportation, medications,

personal-care items and home goods are all things you can buy with student loans.

Types of Student Loans

All student loans can be divided into two major categories: private and federal. It's a good idea to carefully consider which loan type makes the most sense for you, because when it comes time to make payments, the requirements can be quite different.

Federal student loans are made through programs administered by the U.S. government. These loans are generally more borrower-friendly than private loans and don't require payments while you're still a full-time student. After graduation, some federal loans also offer grace periods, allowing you to postpone making payments until you've secured employment. If you choose to defer, you may end up paying more overall, but it can be a helpful option if you're struggling to make payments.

Undergraduate students with qualifying financial need can get a subsidized federal student loan, in which case the subsidy covers the interest while they're in school. Interest begins to accrue right away on unsubsidized federal loans, which aren't based on financial need.

PRO
TIP

You can use student loans to help pay for living expenses like books, school supplies, groceries and gas or bus fare, as well as tuition.

The type of loan you get can impact your payment plans after graduation.

If you're not eligible, or federal loans don't cover all your costs, private student loans are the next option to consider. Private student loans come from lenders such as banks or credit unions. Some private lenders require you to begin paying back your loans before you've finished school. And if you don't make those payments, you may be hit with penalties and damage to your credit score.

Applying for Loans

So, how do you get student loans in the first place? Your initial step in the loan process is to fill out the Free Application for Federal Student Aid, also known as the FAFSA. This form will help determine which federal loans you might qualify for. (You can find the FAFSA online at studentaid.ed.gov.) If you're not eligible for

Student debt can often follow you for many years after you leave school.

own credit. Parents can also take out loans to help pay for their child's education. PLUS loans are the federal loans available to parents, and some private lenders offer loans just for parents to borrow. For the federal loan, parents must submit a FAFSA with their child, in addition to a PLUS loan application.

Paying Off Your Loans

Tackling student debt after college can be a big challenge. While college degrees do often equate to higher salaries, college grads typically don't land high-paying jobs right out of school. For that reason, various repayment plans exist and can help you pay off those student loans while still juggling other expenses.

Depending on the loans you choose, you may be able to work out a new repayment plan or apply to use deferment or forbearance options to reduce or postpone your loan payments. Students who have accrued federal student debt but who go into public service careers may qualify for certain loan-forgiveness programs.

Your repayment options will depend largely on your lender, so investigate your different options carefully and consider how you'll manage student debt after graduation.

federal loans, or the federal loans won't cover all of your anticipated college expenses, you can also apply for private student loans directly through a lender. Private loans will often require a co-signer if a student hasn't built enough of his or her

WHY THE FAFSA MATTERS

The FAFSA can help you request financial aid and find out how much loan and grant assistance you qualify for from colleges, states and the federal government. It's worth taking the time to fill it out, even if you think your income is too high.

Don't assume you won't qualify for any financial aid—in 2018, all undergraduates who were dependents qualified for at least $27,000 in unsubsidized federal Stafford loans over a four-year period—no matter their family's income level.

To determine your financial need, the FAFSA takes into account your cost of attendance at a given school and your family's expected contribution, which is estimated as 20% of the student's assets plus 5.64% of the parents' assets.

Each year, the FAFSA can be filled out online starting October 1. It's important to complete it as close to that date as possible; states and schools often have limited loans and grants available, and these may be issued on a first-come-first-served basis.

WHAT'S DIFFERENT ABOUT FEDERAL STUDENT LOANS? Government-sponsored loans offer some advantages over private ones, including forgiveness programs (depending on your career)

If you're paying for college for yourself or your child, you've got lots of options, from grants and scholarships to federal and private loans. But when it comes to borrowing money for college, how do federal loans differ from private loans?

For starters, federal student loans tend to offer more options for repayment and deferment than private student loans do. And unlike private lenders, federal loan programs will sometimes grant loan forgiveness to qualifying borrowers in certain occupations.

Qualifying for Federal Loans

If you or your child is considering taking out student loans, it's important to note that not everyone is eligible for federal student loans, but people often qualify even when they didn't expect to. So it's worth filling out the Free Application for Federal Student Aid, more commonly known as the FAFSA—the form that determines whether you're eligible to receive federal financial aid.

Federal students loans can be more accessible to some students than private loans. That's because while federal loan programs typically consider financial need, most of them don't require a credit check. They also don't require a co-signer, which many private lenders ask for.

Filling out the FAFSA is often the first step in determining eligibility for federal student loans.

There are three basic types of federal student loans: direct subsidized, direct unsubsidized and PLUS loans. Direct subsidized loans are for qualifying undergraduate students with financial need, while direct unsubsidized loans are for qualifying undergrad, graduate and professional students regardless of financial need. PLUS loans are for qualifying parents of undergraduate students, or graduate or professional students. These loans aren't based on financial need, but they do require a credit check.

85

Paying Off Federal Student Loans

With the exception of PLUS loans, all federal loans offer a grace period before borrowers must start making payments. This grace period—usually lasting at least six months after you graduate—can be important for students who are job-hunting, relocating and transitioning into their new careers after college.

Another bonus: Federal loans offer a variety of repayment plans that you can potentially change, depending on your circumstances. For example, some plans adapt to make your payments more affordable based on your income and family size.

Some federal student loans also allow for deferment and forbearance when a borrower meets certain conditions, such as serving in the Peace Corps or becoming unemployed.

Loan Forgiveness

For students going into public service or teaching careers, federal loans carry an even bigger appeal, because borrowers who end up working for qualifying employers may be eligible for loan forgiveness. That means the borrower is no longer responsible for paying back their debt.

Keep in mind, only federal direct loans can be forgiven after 10 years' worth of payments. But for the Public Service Loan Forgiveness Program, qualifying employers may include government agencies and some nonprofits that provide public services.

More Options for Borrowers

Private loans can be a useful next step when you've exhausted your federal loan options. And private loans sometimes offer lower interest rates than federal loans to students and parents—or students with co-signers—who have good credit scores.

It is true that you could get a lower interest rate with a private loan; however, federal loan programs offer some benefits that you won't find with private lenders.

If you go into public service or teaching, your federal loan may be eligible for forgiveness or cancellation.

CONSOLIDATING YOUR STUDENT LOANS
A strategy to simplify, and maybe even lower, your monthly payments

It can be tricky to juggle multiple student loans. At best, making sure each loan is paid each month takes extra time and effort. At worst, some of those payments fall through the cracks—meaning more time and effort fixing the problem. Consolidating your student loans can be a useful way to more easily manage your debt.

Before consolidating your loans, there are a few things to know. If you have a mix of federal and private loans, you may want to follow different steps to consolidate each type. Understand the benefits and protections you may get from your loans before jumping into the consolidation process.

Private Student Loans

Private student loans are consolidated by refinancing with a private lender. You take out a brand new education loan, which you use to pay off the balances of your current loans. You may qualify for a lower interest rate, particularly if your credit score or financial situation has improved since you first took out the loans. You also may be able to choose the length of the loan.

The Benefits of a Fixed Interest Rate

A variable-rate loan may look attractive—the rates on these loans often are lower than fixed-rate loans at the beginning of the loan. But over time the loan's rate can rise, meaning your monthly payment may jump sharply higher after a few months. Those unpredictable payments can make it more difficult to build a debt-management plan. As a result, a fixed-rate loan may be your best bet for refinancing. The initial interest rate may be a little bit higher than the initial rate on a variable loan, but the fixed rate won't rise over time, giving you a more dependable monthly payment.

Federal Student Loans

The refinancing process for federal student loans is different than with a private loan. Federal loans are refinanced through the Department of Education, and the interest rate of a federal consolidation student loan is calculated according to a strict formula. The interest rate is always fixed, and the new consolidation loan retains the protections and repayment options that come with federal student loans.

If you have Federal Family Education, Perkins or parent PLUS loans, you may need to consolidate before you can take advantage of income-based repayment or public service loan forgiveness. So even if federal loan consolidation doesn't seem appealing on its own merits, it may be a key step in taming your debt.

There is no up-front fee to consolidate your federal loans, so beware of a company that tries to charge you to help with consolidation. Visit studentloans.gov to fill out an application.

One bigger payment can yield bigger payoffs than several smaller ones.

Some private lenders will forbear your loan while you're enrolled in school and for six months after.

TO DEFER OR FORBEAR? You may be able to postpone your student loan payments

If you're struggling to make your student loan payments, it may be tempting to just put away the checkbook and take a break from paying those bills.

And here's the good news: You may be able to do just that—without the risk of defaulting on your loans. By receiving a deferment or forbearance, you can potentially put a temporary halt to your loan repayments.

Before you jump into a deferment or forbearance, take the time to understand how each works—and whether you're eligible for one or both options.

Deferment

Deferment is the ideal way to postpone your loan payments, but it's generally only available on federal student loans. When you defer subsidized federal loans, interest stops accruing. That means that at the end of the deferment period, your balance won't have grown. You've effectively extended the term of your loan without increasing the amount you pay back.

Unsubsidized loans, on the other hand, will accrue interest during deferment. Your balance will grow while your loan is deferred. When you restart, you will be making payments on that larger balance, which means you will end up paying more over the life of the loan. For unsubsidized loans, it's often recommended to make reduced payments during deferment that just cover the accruing interest. If you can afford it, you'll save money in the long run.

Your federal loans are deferred for as long as you, or the student on whose behalf you took out the loan, are enrolled at least half-time at an eligible school and for six months afterward. (If you don't automatically receive the deferment, contact your school, which will send the necessary information to your loan servicer.)

You otherwise may be eligible for deferment if you are enrolled in an approved rehabilitation training program for the disabled; unemployed or underemployed; experiencing economic hardship; or on active military duty. In some cases, these deferments are only good for up to three years.

Forbearance

If deferment is not available, you may be able to postpone or reduce payments through a forbearance. This is usually the only option available for private student loans. (Your private lender may use the words "defer" and "forbear" interchangeably.)

> Deferment is the ideal way to postpone your loan payments, but it's generally only available on federal student loans.

If you're not paying off your loan, you are likely continuing to pay interest.

All loans in forbearance accrue interest, whether they are private or federal, subsidized or unsubsidized. As with a deferment, you can opt to make interest payments during forbearance. In fact, some lenders may require it.

When you meet certain criteria, you may request a mandatory forbearance on your federal loan that your servicer is legally bound to grant. Those criteria vary based on the type of loan, but can include your monthly student loan obligations exceeding 20% of your gross income; serving in the Peace Corps or AmeriCorps; completing a medical or dental internship or residency; and serving actively in the National Guard.

Otherwise, you may request a discretionary forbearance—which, as its name implies, is granted at the discretion of your loan servicer. Discretionary forbearances are typically granted

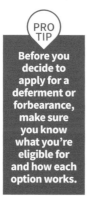

PRO TIP

Before you decide to apply for a deferment or forbearance, make sure you know what you're eligible for and how each option works.

for only a few months at a time. Some private lenders will forbear your loan while you are enrolled in school and for six months after you are no longer enrolled. An in-school forbearance may run out after a certain number of years, whether you are still enrolled or not. You can sometimes request a forbearance or a partial forbearance from your private lender because of financial hardship or unemployment.

Things to Remember When Applying

The first thing to remember when considering deferment or forbearance is that you typically are not eligible for either if your loan is already in default. That's why it's important to apply before falling behind on your payments. And once you've applied, make sure you keep paying until the deferment or forbearance is in place. Even if you meet the criteria for a mandatory postponement, it might not kick in automatically. Contact your loan servicer directly to begin the process. Be prepared to provide proof that you meet the relevant criteria for the deferment or forbearance.

HOW TO CHOOSE A STUDENT LOAN
Shopping around means looking at more than interest rates

Figuring out how to pay for college can sometimes make getting accepted seem like the easy part. If you need a loan, don't worry—you're in good company. Nearly seven in 10 students who graduated in the class of 2018 had an average debt of around $30,000 when they received their degrees.

Here's what to consider as you shop around for student loans.

Compare Interest Rates

Interest rates heavily contribute to the total cost of a loan. In a nutshell, the higher the interest rate, the more your loan will cost you. Federal loans feature fixed rates set annually by Congress. That means the interest rate you see when you take out the loan will be the rate you pay until you refinance your loan or pay it off. The interest rates on Federal Direct Loans issued to undergraduates usually compare favorably to others on the market. Interest rates tend to be higher on Federal PLUS loans issued to graduate students and parents, however.

Private loans can offer any interest rate they want, but be careful: You or any co-borrower will likely need an excellent credit rating to get the lowest rate advertised. Variable-rate loans may also look tempting, but a low rate today could wind up being significantly higher in the future if interest rates go up.

Look for Flexible Payback Terms

All federal loans and some private loans will allow you to hit the pause button on your loan repayments through either deferment or forbearance. Federal loans offer deferments in specific situations where your long-term ability to make payments is affected—for example, if you decide to continue going to school. If you have a federal

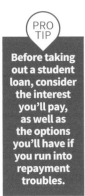

PRO TIP

Before taking out a student loan, consider the interest you'll pay, as well as the options you'll have if you run into repayment troubles.

If you decide that you want to go to graduate school, it's possible to put off the payments of your federally funded undergraduate loans.

subsidized loan, you won't be charged any interest while you're in a deferment period. For all other loans, however, your lender will continue to charge interest and your loan balance will continue to grow while you're not making payments on it.

Know Your Loan-Forgiveness Options

If you run into trouble making payments, federal loans also offer an income-driven repayment option. If you qualify, your payment becomes a set percentage of your income. If you still owe money after 20 to 25 years of lower payments, the government will forgive the remainder of the loan. Keep in mind that your interest rate won't change, so you'll pay more in interest over the life of your loan in this scenario.

Federal loans also let you take advantage of the Public Service Loan Forgiveness Program, which offers loan forgiveness as an incentive to pursue careers that benefit society. You'll need to make regular payments and keep an eligible job at least 30 hours a week for 10 years in order to qualify for forgiveness, so it may be worth checking out an income-driven repayment option to reduce your overall financial burden.

The average U.S. household with student debt owes about $47,600.

Consumer Debt

From car loans to medical bills,
a look at smart ways to handle
paying for our everyday expenses

AUTO LOAN BASICS Shopping for the right car also means shopping for the right loan

The average price of a new car is $37,000. The median annual income for American workers is $63,000. With numbers like that, it's easy to see why very few consumers can pay cash for a new vehicle. And that's why buying a new car often means first heading to the bank to take out a loan.

Applying for a Loan

Auto loans are secured, so they can be easier to get than some other types of loans—even if your credit isn't so great. Here's why: In the same way that your house serves as collateral for your mortgage, the car serves as collateral for your auto loan. If you stop making payments, the lender can recoup some of that money by repossessing your car. And because these loans are a safer bet for lenders, interest rates tend to be lower than on unsecured debt, such as credit cards. These days, the average loan for a new car has an interest rate between 4% and 5%.

Where to Get a Loan

The first place many people look for an auto loan is at the dealership itself. If the dealership does financing, they'll offer you some loan options. Each loan will have an interest rate (the APR) and a term, a set length of time over which you'll be paying off the loan, usually between two and six years.

But before you accept the dealership's terms, shop around, because you may get a better deal else-where. Talk to your bank's lending department and check out online networks that specialize in auto loans. If you get a great offer from one of these sources, bring it to the dealer. They may want to beat the offer with a better interest rate, or knock down the car's price if you're willing to finance through them.

Another way to improve your loan terms is with a large down payment. While many people consider 20% an appropriate down payment for a car, more is always better. A higher down payment will decrease your monthly payments and the amount of interest you pay over time, and it can persuade lenders to offer you more favorable terms.

Before signing up for an auto loan, shop around to make sure you're getting the best deal.

Loan Terms

Consider the terms of a loan carefully before buying. Today, the average loan for a new car is 72 months, or six years. The average amount of time that people keep that new car is 6.5 years. In other words, the average person buying a new car today will only own their car outright for six months before moving on to their next vehicle. Sure, longer loan terms mean lower monthly payments, but because of interest, you'll end up paying more than the price of the car over time. If you need a low monthly payment and don't plan to keep your car for a long time, leasing may be a good option to consider.

> In the same way that your house serves as collateral for your mortgage, the car serves as collateral for your auto loan. If you stop making payments, the lender can recoup some of that money by repossessing your car.

you purchased it, you may have a hard time refinancing.

Selling a Financed Car

Longer loans also limit your options if you want to sell your car but still have payments left to make. Essentially, you'll have to pay off the car in order to sell it. For example, say you still owe $3,000 on your car, but you're ready to sell it. You have a buyer, but they're only willing to pay $2,000. In order to sell the car to that buyer, you'll have to hand the lender that $2,000, plus another $1,000 of your own, to pay off the loan.

One nice thing about auto loans is that you can refinance them at any time. If you improve your credit score, ask your lender to refinance so you can get a better interest rate. But remember that cars are depreciable assets—which means they lose value over time. In fact, cars lose 22% of their value in their first year. If your car has lost significant value since

Another option is a trade-in: When you trade in a car, you sell it back to a dealer—often at a lower price than in a private sale—and put any profit toward a new loan on a different car.

Before signing up for an auto loan, shop around to make sure you're getting the best deal.

WHEN YOUR OTHER CAR IS NOT A CAR

You can also get a loan to purchase other types of vehicles—boats, RVs, tractors and even small planes.

First, figure out your budget. Remember that you'll have to pay for maintenance, repair and, in some cases, monthly storage, hangar or docking fees. Factor in these costs when you're considering what you can afford.

Next, investigate your financing options. Make an appointment at your bank or credit union to see if they offer loans for that vehicle. Also ask the dealer or manufacturer if they offer financing. You may find attractive loan terms from the companies that make and sell RVs and boats. Some lenders specialize in certain vehicles, too: For instance, many farmers depend on lenders who only finance tractors and agricultural equipment. And pilots associations often work with lenders who finance small aircraft.

Loans for these other types of vehicles tend to be secured by the vehicles themselves. Banks view them as less risky. That's because they can always repossess that vehicle if you fail to make payments. So, no matter how much you love your two seater Cessna, you definitely won't be flying high for long if you stop making your payments.

BUYING VS. LEASING A CAR When you've got your eye on a new ride, what's the best option for you?

When you're in the market for a new car, you generally have two options: buy or lease. The right choice for you depends on your preferences and your financial situation.

The Differences Between Owning and Leasing

When you buy a car, you own it—for better or for worse. You can put 50,000 miles on it in the first year, paint it orange and sell it whenever you want. You also get to determine the level of insurance you want to pay for. When you lease a car, none of this applies. Your lease will specify how many miles you're allowed to drive—with steep costs per additional mile—and the amount of insurance you'll have to carry.

Ownership also means you're responsible for all maintenance and repairs. New cars come with limited warranties. If your warranty has expired and your alternator goes kaput, you're looking at a $500 trip to the mechanic, in addition to any regular monthly loan payment you might have. With a lease, you can expect most repairs to be covered under warranty—but do read the lease agreement's fine print to be sure. You should still expect to cover routine maintenance like oil changes and tire rotation on leased vehicles.

Leasing a car can be a good choice for people operating with tight budgets.

Do the Math

Generally, the monthly cost to lease a vehicle tends to be significantly lower than auto loan payments you'd make if you bought the car. That's because your monthly payment reflects the depreation of the car while it's in your hands. Cars are depreciating assets, which means they lose value every year. You also won't have to save up for a large down payment (and you might not need one at all if your credit is good). This can make leasing significantly more affordable for those who struggle with monthly cash flow but still need a reliable vehicle. Over time, however, buying a car can make more financial sense. When you lease a vehicle, you always have a monthly payment to make, and you'll never have a car that's actually yours. But when you take out a loan to buy a car, every monthly payment you make buys you more equity in that vehicle. And once the loan is paid off, you get to keep driving the car without worrying about making monthly loan payments.

Read the Fine Print

At the end of your lease term, you simply turn in the car and walk away, right? Well, sort of. Dealerships are notorious for the high cost of additional mileage and for tacking on questionable repairs. Every scratch and stain may cost you something when you turn in a leased car. And you'll likely be penalized if you want to end your lease early.

One way to avoid the sky-high cost for additional mileage is to ask up front for a high-mileage lease. These types of leases are rarely advertised, but many lenders still offer them. Your monthly payment will be higher since you're putting more wear and tear on the car, but this kind of lease will protect you in the event of an unexpected road trip or if you have a high-mileage commute.

PRO TIP

Loved driving your leased car? You may be able to buy your vehicle at the end of your contract— sometimes for less than it's worth.

Just because a lease is in essence a rental, it doesn't mean it's not considered debt. Credit reporting agencies and potential lenders see your lease as a recurring payment, or a liability. Other lenders will take both the payment amount and your payment history into account when deciding whether or not to lend to you.

When you purchase a car, you are gaining some equity.

THE INS AND OUTS OF PAYDAY LOANS
These loans offer a short-term fix, but can also cause long-term financial problems

We've all been in the situation of scrimping pennies until our next paycheck, but what do you do when the bills are due before your next check arrives? In these situations, you might be tempted by payday loans, which promise immediate credit to those who need cash in a hurry. But these loans can trap consumers in endless cycles of debt, so borrowers should be extremely careful when using them.

What Is a Payday Loan?
A payday loan is a short-term, high-interest loan for a relatively small amount of money, usually a few hundred dollars. The borrower repays the loan, and its interest, in one lump sum upon receipt of their next paycheck. These loans often last no more than a few weeks and are meant only to serve as a cash cushion until the borrower gets more funds. The application process is simple, quick and doesn't require a full credit check, making these loans especially tempting for those with nonexistent or bad credit.

Beware High Interest
On the surface, payday loans don't seem so bad, but payday lenders often charge incredibly high interest rates. For example, a two-week payday loan with a typical $15 fee per every $100 borrowed equates to an annual percentage rate (APR) of nearly 400%. This is far greater than the typical APR on credit cards, which range from about 15% to 25%. Payday loans are so risky that many states heavily regulate them, and some states, including New York and New Jersey, simply don't allow them.

To repay the loan, payday lenders typically require borrowers to write (at the time of the loan) post-dated checks for both the loan amount and the interest charged, set to coincide with the borrower's payroll deposit. This ensures the lender receives the payment by a scheduled date and doesn't have to chase the borrower to receive it.

The trap comes at the time of repayment. Say, for example, someone living paycheck to paycheck with no savings has car trouble they can't afford to fix. They need the car to get to work, so they take out a payday loan of $500 for repairs and write the loan company a check for $575—the amount of the loan plus interest. However, the chances of coming up with $575 in two weeks may be pretty slim. In these cases, consumers can end up taking out another loan to pay for the first and so on until they find themselves in a cycle of debt they can't escape. If a borrower can't repay the loan, the payday lender can sue them and even garnish their wages, taking money directly from their paycheck until the debt is paid.

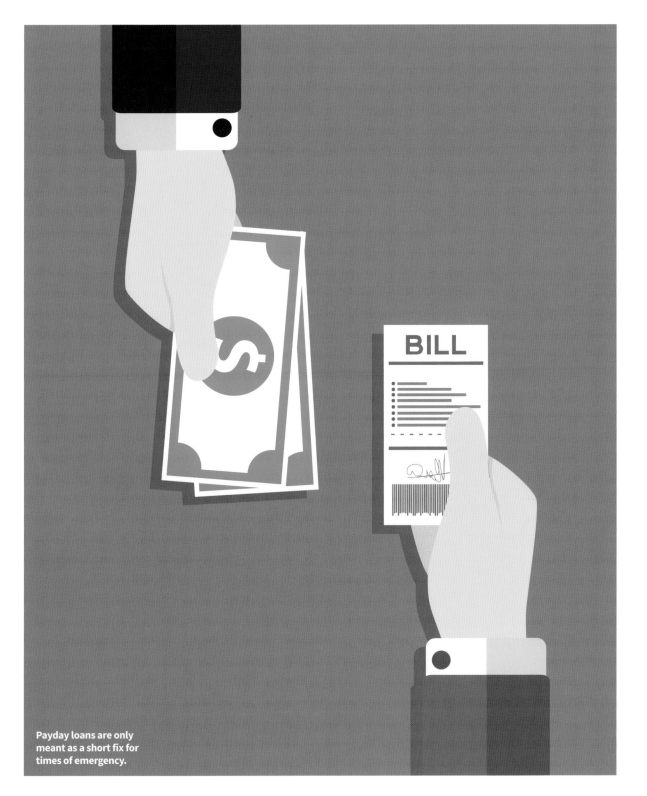

Payday loans are only meant as a short fix for times of emergency.

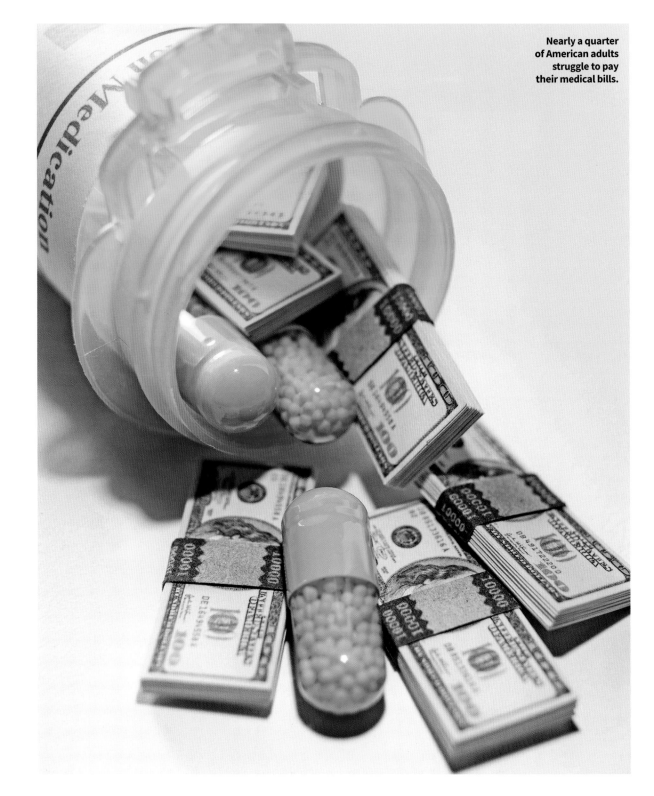

Nearly a quarter of American adults struggle to pay their medical bills.

UNDERSTANDING MEDICAL DEBT
Get well soon…now here's your bill

In the United States, medical care—whether it's emergency surgery or prescriptions for a chronic condition—can come at a high cost. An unexpected illness or accident can leave you saddled with an overwhelming amount of debt, even if you have insurance. In fact, more than 25% of American adults between 18 and 64 struggle to pay medical bills. But medical debt doesn't have to take over your life. It can often be negotiated down, paid off according to your income or sometimes even wiped out.

Before You Start Paying It Off

Many people don't realize that medical debt can often be negotiated. Before you make your first payment, check your bill against the figures in the Healthcare Bluebook, a free online guide that lists the average costs for medical procedures. If your bill seems much higher than it should be, point this out to the billing department. You can also ask to pay the rate that Medicaid or Medicare would pay for the same care—which could lower the bill quite a bit.

Another tactic may be to make a large payment up front. Let the billing department know that you are willing to pay a sizeable amount of your tab immediately if they are willing to write off a significant chunk of the bill. If you have a tough time advocating for yourself, you may want to hire a medical-billing advocate, who can negotiate on your behalf.

Making Payments Affordable

For bills larger than what you can pay immediately, ask the billing department about payment plan options. Ask for one that is interest-free and structured around your income level. Let them know what you can afford and ask them to work with you.

Some credit card providers offer medical credit cards, and many also have a zero-interest introductory period. However, if you need longer to pay off your debt, the interest can add up quickly.

If you absolutely need to, you can apply for a loan through a bank or other lender to pay off medical debt. However, you'll have to pay interest on these loans, which will ultimately make the bill more expensive as that interest accumulates.

What If You Can't Pay?

If you can't pay, first apply for financial assistance. Caseworkers can help you apply for Medicaid. If you don't qualify, they may be able to help you access charity care or other financial assistance.

Also, be honest with debt collectors about what you can pay—even if it's a small amount. Don't offer more than you can realistically afford, or you may end up trapped in a debt cycle that's hard to escape.

PRO TIP

Clinics and hospitals often have caseworkers who can help you apply for Medicaid, which can assist with debt you can't afford.

107

AVOID MEDICAL DEBT WITH A HEALTH SAVINGS ACCOUNT How this specialized savings account can make medical expenses more affordable

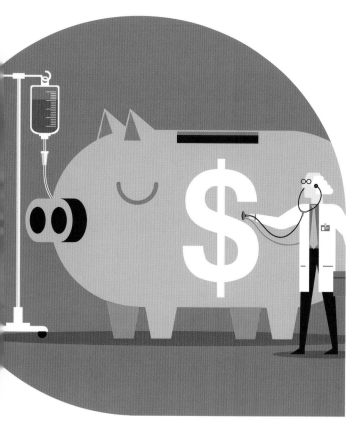

Whether it's one unexpected trip to the emergency room or managing a long-term medical condition, medical expenses can wreak havoc on your financial plans and send you into debt. Putting a portion of your paycheck into a Health Savings Account (HSA) can help you save for medical expenses, making you more prepared if you are hit with big medical bills.

What Is a Health Savings Account?

Health Savings Accounts, or HSAs, are specialized savings accounts that are designed to offer a tax-advantaged way to cover out-of-pocket medical expenses. Contributions are made pre-tax (or are tax-deductible if made outside of payroll deductions), and you can make tax-free withdrawals to pay for qualified medical expenses such as doctor's office co-pays, prescription costs and hospital visits.

HSA Advantages

Prescription medications, hospital stays or surgeries can be really expensive, but HSAs can help make medical expenses more affordable. Unlike the use-it-or-lose-it provisions of flexible spending accounts (FSAs), HSAs allow your savings and earnings to accumulate from year to year, meaning you can build and maintain a medical expense fund to tap

PRO TIP

HSAs are tax-advantaged—contributions are made with pre-tax earnings or are tax deductible—helping you save money at tax time.

HSAs are designed to help you save money for medical expenses.

into when the unexpected happens. Using HSA savings to cover medical expenses can also effectively discount their overall cost, since every dollar spent hasn't been reduced by taxes.

How to Start and Use an HSA

Check with your health insurance provider to see if your plan qualifies for an HSA. If your insurance provider doesn't offer an HSA, you can open one through a bank, a credit union or through an online HSA provider. Once your account is set up, you will receive a debit card or checks that are linked to your HSA balance to pay for qualified medical expenses, such as deductibles and co-pays. You also can pay those costs out of pocket and reimburse yourself from your HSA account.

Check with your health insurance provider to see if your plan qualifies for an HSA.

The Bottom Line

HSAs are powerful tools that can help mitigate medical costs, keep your budget in line, and provide new opportunities to save for your future. A little pre-planning and additional savings now can make all the difference in the long run when it comes to your medical debt.

HSAs provide a tax-advantaged way to help you cover your medical bills.

THE PROS AND CONS OF PERSONAL LOANS
Personal loans can be used for everything from launching your own business to paying down credit card debt

Say you're staring at a hefty price tag for a wedding or some pricey new appliances, and you don't have the savings on hand. How will you cover those costs? A personal loan might be the answer you're looking for—as long as you also understand the risks.

A personal loan is money from a lender that you receive in a lump sum and then pay back with interest over a set term—typically up to five years. Interest rates, which depend on factors such as your credit rating, typically vary from 6% to as high as 36%. Personal loans are unsecured, meaning they have no collateral to back them. As a result, personal loans often carry higher interest rates than secured loans.

> **PRO TIP**
> Read the fine print on personal loans. Some carry hefty costs, such as origination fees that can increase the price you end up paying.

As with most loans, lenders will take a look at your debt history before offering you a loan. A lender will decide your loan eligibility, amount and interest rate after evaluating your debt-to-income ratio and credit report. If you don't qualify for a personal loan, a lender may offer a secured loan, or allow you to take out a loan with a co-signer. Applying for a loan with a bank where you're already a customer can sometimes help you secure better rates, and your bank may be able to recommend a type of loan that fits your needs.

Ways to Use a Personal Loan
You can use a personal loan to finance almost anything you can imagine: a new boat, new furniture, a wedding, outstanding medical bills, an expensive gift or the start-up of your own business, for example. In most cases, you're free to spend personal loan funds as you see fit.

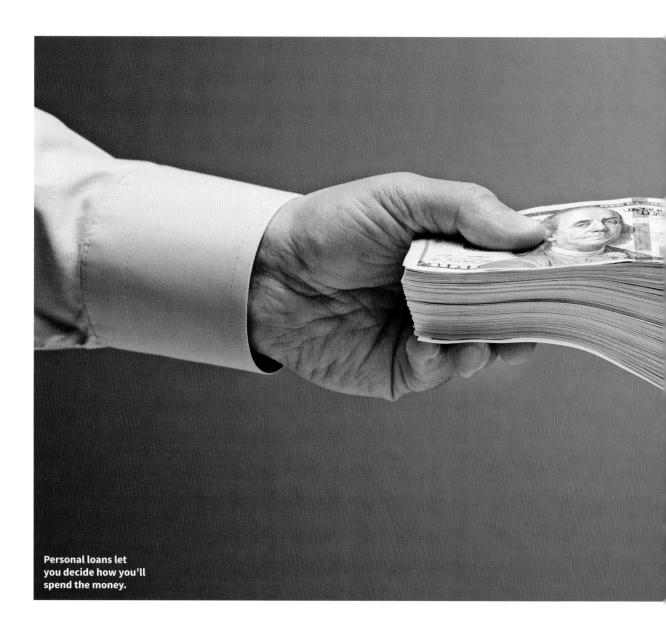

Personal loans let you decide how you'll spend the money.

A personal loan can also be used to consolidate debts, so instead of paying off multiple high credit card balances at once, you could make just one payment at a (hopefully) lower rate. Personal loans can also be a smart way to refinance your student debt, because personal loans often carry lower interest rates than student loans. However, they won't offer

You can use a personal loan to finance almost anything you can imagine.

the tax advantages that come with some student loans.

Watch Out for the Downside

While a personal loan can be useful in a number of situations, there are potential drawbacks to be aware of when using a personal loan. Applying for personal loans, and the timeliness of your payments, affects your credit

score. If you fall behind on your payments, your credit score may suffer.

Also, you will pay a fee just for taking out the loan. The origination fee typically is calculated as a percentage of your total loan amount, and this fee often ranges from 1% to 8%. Another financial risk is that getting ahead on payments may not be allowed. In fact, you may actually incur a prepayment penalty if you try to pay off your loan early.

Before you apply for a loan, look into your lender carefully, since scammers sometimes target would-be borrowers. If you have doubt about a lender's trustworthiness, consult the Consumer Financial Protection Bureau (consumerfinance.gov).

Research your options and decide on the plan that works best for you. Take the time to consider your needs and your ability to make payments, and borrow only what you can realistically afford to repay.

HOW TO HANDLE—AND AVOID—TAX DEBT
The longer you wait to pay the IRS, the steeper the consequences you'll face

Tax debt typically begins when you fail to pay your taxes or when you miss filing your tax return. Living under the cloud of tax debt is stressful in no small part because this form of debt doesn't go away until you pay it off—even, in most cases, if you file for bankruptcy.

If you've skipped filing your return for one or more years, it's possible the IRS won't catch on right away. But when the agency does take notice, it has some very effective methods for chasing down payment that can cause tremendous headaches for the delinquent taxpayer.

Immediate Penalties

If you've fallen behind on your taxes because you don't have the means to pay—or because you've simply chosen not to pay—your amount due will immediately start to grow, thanks to interest. The interest rate is based on the federal short-term rate, and for the last quarter of 2019, it was 5%.

In addition to racking up interest, the IRS will charge you a failure-to-pay penalty if you don't meet your tax obligations. If you haven't paid 90% of your taxes by the tax deadline, the IRS will apply a penalty of 0.5% to 1% of the unpaid amount. This penalty will be applied each month up to 25%.

If you didn't file your tax return, you'll face a failure-to-file penalty. In this case, the IRS will tack on a penalty equal to 5% of the unpaid amount each month until it reaches a maximum of 25%. If you can explain why you filed late, the IRS may reduce the penalties.

Long-Term Results of Failing to Pay

Unfortunately, the consequences of not paying your taxes only get worse as time goes on. If you fail to pay in the long term, the IRS can garnish your wages. The IRS will take a cut of your paycheck—paying the government back before those wages even get to you.

The IRS can also attempt to recover the amount you owe by seizing assets, such as cars, boats, real estate or even the money in your bank account. And the agency can place a lien on your house or

> If you've fallen behind on your taxes because you don't have the means to pay—or because you've simply chosen not to pay—your amount due will immediately start to grow, thanks to interest.

One thing is certain: The IRS will find out if you fail to pay your taxes.

other property, which prevents you from selling it before you've paid back your taxes.

In addition to these material consequences, tax debt leaves a stain on your credit report, making it difficult to qualify for future loans and credit lines. Tax liens in particular can have a lasting effect on your reputation with lenders.

Tax debt alone usually doesn't result in criminal charges or jail time. The government typically reserves criminal prosecution for people committing tax fraud—hiding documents and concealing their actual income to avoid paying what they owe—or continually failing to file tax returns. Although criminal charges are relatively rare, if you do wind up in court over unpaid taxes, the legal process can be very costly.

How to Pay off Tax Debt

If you are behind on your taxes, first, find out if you qualify for an IRS payment plan. If you're eligible, you may be able to get a six-month extension for paying off your taxes. If you need longer than six months, the IRS may allow you to repay your debt with a monthly payment plan. For taxpayers who can demonstrate that pay-

ing their tax debt would be seriously harmful to their finances, the IRS may approve an offer in compromise. Along with your application, you must submit 20% of your offer amount up front, plus a nonrefundable fee. If the IRS accepts your offer, your payments can be made monthly or in a lump sum.

If you're facing dire financial circumstances and can't pay for anything beyond basic necessities, the IRS may determine you qualify for a deferral. A "Currently Not Collectible" status means the IRS will stop trying to collect, but you'll continue to accrue interest and penalties.

If you don't qualify for a payment plan, consider using credit cards or personal loans to kick the IRS debt. By using a loan, you can avoid additional government penalties.

For large debts, you may want to consult a tax attorney or accountant who can help you sort out your options and work with the IRS on a plan that will best suit your situation.

> **PRO TIP**
> File your taxes every year, even if you can't afford to pay immediately. Failure-to-file penalties are steeper than failure-to-pay penalties.

The IRS can seize assets or garnish your wages to recover owed taxes.

HOW UTILITY BILLS CAN AFFECT YOUR DEBT
Falling behind on utility payments can cause lasting issues, but you can take action to prevent the worst consequences

The bills you pay every month might not seem like debt in the traditional sense. But you owe your utility companies and service providers for the heat, water, electricity and internet your household uses—and those companies, just like credit lenders, expect you to pay. If you can't, your unpaid bills become debt. And if you fall behind on your utility payments, the consequences can be similar to those you face if you fail to make credit card payments.

So, it can be useful to think of bills in the same framework as you consider debt: Your bills are something you should budget for. If you can't afford to pay your bills, seek help and work to resolve the issue as soon as possible.

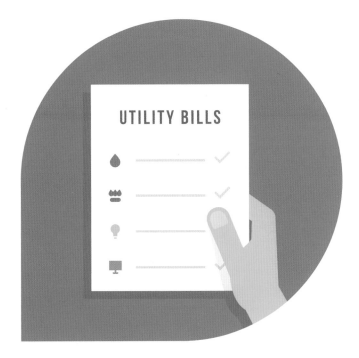

PRO TIP

Your FICO score doesn't include bills, but other credit-scoring companies may include these types of debts in figuring your credit score.

What Happens if You Fall Behind?

Unlike debts you choose to take on—like an auto loan for a new car, for instance—many of your bills are related to services you absolutely need. For example, you likely can't go without heat during a cold winter. This is why it's a good idea to prioritize your utility bills in your monthly budget.

Paying utility bills on time is important because the timeliness of your payments can impact your credit score. While the traditional FICO credit score accounts for your credit card and other debt payments, alternative credit scores may look at your history with utility companies and other service providers. Paying your bills on time can help your credit score with these companies, in some cases, and failing to pay on time will hurt you.

117

If you fall behind on your utility bills and your debt is turned over to a collection agency, your debt will go on your record with credit bureaus, damaging your main credit score. Your track record with utility companies can also affect your ability to get utilities in the future. If you have a history of failing to pay, you may have to put down a big deposit to start an account with a new provider.

How to Get Help

If you can't pay your bills, your first step should be contacting your utility providers to let them know you're having financial difficulty. Contact them in order of importance—ensuring your water and power stay on before you talk to other companies, such as your internet provider. When you're proactive, providers will often work with you to find solutions. They may be able to average your monthly bills, for example, lowering the amount you owe right now.

If you're struggling to pay bills, you can also look for assistance from federal and state programs and nonprofits that offer aid in a crisis. Just as programs exist to help borrowers who are struggling with mortgage payments or student loans, there are programs that can help you manage your bill payments if you're falling behind.

Another strategy for digging out from under a pile of bills is to eliminate any unnecessary services. You may be able to lower your bills by cutting cable and streaming services, or shopping around for cheaper car insurance. It's also easy to forget about subscriptions and club memberships you signed up for in the past, so review your bank and credit card statements to see if any can be canceled.

When you're between jobs or if you are facing a financial emergency, it's tempting to avoid the many bold-lettered notices you might receive. Yet, the best way forward is contacting your utility companies and searching for solutions as soon as possible.

If you fall behind on your utility payments, the consequences can be similar to those you face if you fail to make your credit card payments.

PAYMENT DUE

Unpaid utility bills can result in a loss of services.

SECTION

07

Paying Off Debt

Identifying the strategies and help
you need to become debt-free

WHY PAY OFF DEBT Paying down what you owe is no picnic, but neither is the alternative

Carrying debt is stressful. In fact, about a quarter of Americans experience such high levels of money-related stress that researchers have coined the term AFS, or acute financial stress, to describe the way debt and other financial worries can affect mental and physical health. Whether you find yourself overwhelmed by debt or not, it's a good idea to pay it off quickly—even if that requires short-term sacrifices.

Here's a look at some of the benefits of paying down your debt:

● **Own What You Have** For many people, the appeal of paying off debt is being able to own their assets outright. Whether it's a car or a home, it's difficult to feel like you really own something when you're still making payments on it every month. Once you own something free and clear, you can more easily make decisions on when to sell it and for how much. And no one can repossess it for nonpayment.

● **Spend on Things You Love, Not on Interest** When you only make the minimum payments each month, you ultimately end up paying more over time. In the long run, that means you actually have less to spend on the things you love. But once you're out of debt, you'll have that much more income to spend how you please.

> **PRO TIP**
> When you pay off debt, you can put extra cash to work in your savings, or earn returns in tax-advantaged retirement accounts.

It may require some serious discipline now, but you'll have far more freedom later.

● **Gain Financial Security** Paying off as much of your debt as you can now will make a difference to your bottom line down the road, helping you avoid ballooning future liabilities. Because while it may not seem like a big deal to be paying off credit card debt in your 30s and 40s, you most definitely don't want to be paying those bills when you hit retirement age. Escalating bills could prevent you from retiring on time, or could end up taking a big chunk out of a pension or Social Security payments.

● **Protect Your Credit Report** You may think that making regular payments is enough to keep you looking good in the eyes of potential lenders. But when you apply for a loan, banks don't only look at your credit score, they also look at your debt-to-income ratio—or how much debt you're carrying compared to how much money you make. Even if your credit score looks good, if they perceive that you're carrying too much debt, you won't get approved.

● **Avoiding Collections and Bankruptcy** If you stop making payments, your debt may be sent to collections or a lender can seek a judgement against you in court. You can expect plenty of calls from debt collectors—and in the event of a judgment, your wages may be garnished. If you absolutely can't pay it, you may have to declare bankruptcy, a step that shouldn't be taken lightly.

Paying off a little debt now means owing a lot less later.

USE YOUR HEAD AND YOUR HEART TO ELIMINATE DEBT Successful debt-reduction strategies work for your emotions as well as your wallet

Between mortgages, credit cards, auto loans and education loans, Americans are racking up more debt than ever before. Even though the average credit card balance among U.S. households exceeds $4,000, the number of people making late payments has stayed relatively low. But just because you can manage to pay all of your bills on time doesn't mean your current debt load is a good long-term plan.

The problem is, once you get into debt, it can be hard to get out of it. It's easy enough to say you should spend less than you earn, but establishing a budget and sticking to it can be hard work even under the very best of circumstances. If looking at your debt balance gives you a sinking feeling in the pit of your stomach, you're certainly not alone. Being in debt causes stress, which means it takes an emotional and psychological toll. That also means following the cold logic of calculators and budgets often isn't enough to get free of debt. A strategy that accounts for both your financial and psychological health gives you a better chance of sticking to your plan.

> It's easy enough to say you should spend less than you earn, but establishing a budget and sticking to it can be hard work in the best of circumstances.

Start by Taking Stock

Before you formulate a plan, it's time to step back and look at the main factors you can control as you pay off your debts. First, if you find yourself in a hole, take the age-old advice and stop digging. Whether you establish a basic budget or decide to wing it, you'll need to find some source of money to pay off your debts. Once you locate the extra money, it's time to create a plan of attack. Consider one of the three approaches below—or a hybrid approach you can customize to your needs.

Keep It Simple With the Snowflake Strategy

Whether you're not quite ready to take the leap into formal budgeting or you're simply trying to take your existing debt reduction to the next level, the snowflake method can provide a way to make incremental progress.

The snowflake method works by finding lots of little savings that you can put toward one giant goal. Think of money you find in your couch cushions, cash you get for your birthday or income you make from a side gig. Any cash you find

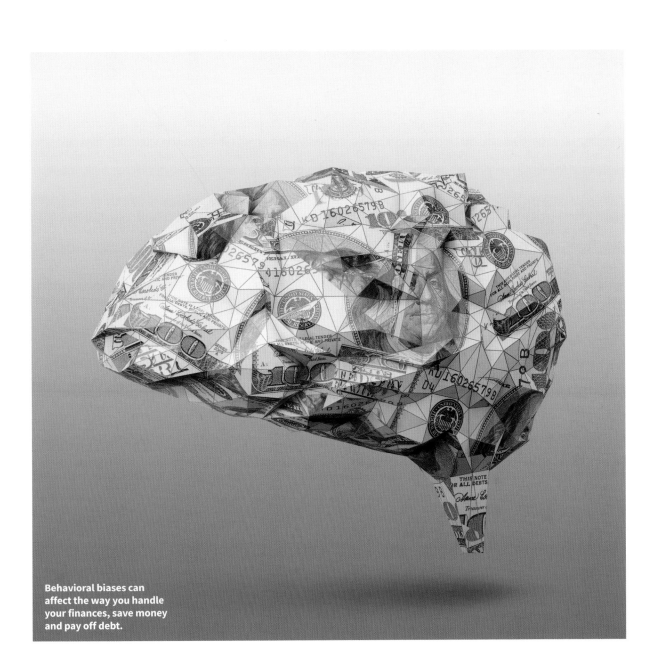

Behavioral biases can affect the way you handle your finances, save money and pay off debt.

that doesn't have a specific purpose in your budget goes into your debt-repayment fund.

The snowflake strategy doesn't require a whole lot of effort to start, but it does require a whole lot of willpower over time to keep it going. That makes it more useful as a way of augmenting a more comprehensive strategy than as a solution on its own.

Targeting High Rates:
The Avalanche Strategy

Once you've got a source of funds ready, it's time to decide which accounts to target first. To pay off your debt as efficiently as possible, you'll want to take a look at the amount of money it costs you to keep making minimum payments on each account. The avalanche method provides an efficient way of paying off your debts by targeting the accounts that cost you the most first.

To use the avalanche method, you'll need to find out the interest rate you pay on each of your debt accounts. Make the minimum payment on all of your accounts first, and then use any additional money to pay off the account with the highest interest rate first. With this method, the actual size of your credit card or loan balance doesn't matter. Once you pay off the balance on the account with the highest rate, you simply move to the account with the next-highest rate.

This method works because it minimizes the amount of interest you pay as you repay your loans. It's logical, and it's efficient. If you can stick to it, you'll save money over almost any other strategy you employ. But sticking to it can be a problem for many people. It can take a long time to get out of debt, especially if your highest-interest debt has a big balance. The avalanche method requires faith in the process and dogged persistence, both of which can be difficult to maintain over the long term.

Rack Up Quick Wins: The Snowball Strategy

Studies looking into the way people deal with multiple debts have found that the human brain just isn't wired properly to pay off debt as efficiently as possible. (That's just one of our brains' failings when it comes to money, in fact.) One of the biggest reasons for that is we crave wins. The snowball strategy may cost more over time than the avalanche strategy, but it gets you off to a quicker start.

To use the snowball strategy, go back to your list of accounts and rank them based on each account's balance. Then pay them off in order, from the

> Like the best diet or exercise plan, in the end, the best debt-reduction strategy is the one you can stick with until you reach your goals. The most efficient strategy in the world won't help if you aren't motivated enough to keep using it.

lowest balance to the highest. If you have higher balances on accounts with high interest rates, this approach will definitely cost more money over time than the avalanche method. Because you start with the lowest balance, however, you pay off the first account sooner. That gives you psychological momentum, making it easier to stick with the strategy over the long term.

Mixing and Matching: Hybrid Strategies

At their roots, the snowball and avalanche strategies play to opposite poles of the human brain. The avalanche appeals to logic, while the snowball appeals more to emotion. You may find yourself somewhere in between those poles. In that case, you might try to start your debt reduction with a card that combines a relatively high rate with a relatively low balance, giving you the emotional boost of reaching your first milestone quickly without giving up the advantages of attacking higher-interest debt early in the process.

You also may find other criteria to use when you rank your debts. If some debt balances cause you more stress and anxiety than others, you may want to pay them off sooner and reap the psychological benefits. For some people, those debts might be the ones with the largest balances or the ones that have been sitting there the longest.

Finding the Best Fit for You

The best debt-reduction strategy is the one you can stick with until you reach your goals. It may even take some experimentation to see what gives you enough momentum to reach the next landmark on your path to becoming debt-free. As the little wins become bigger wins, imagine how good it will feel when you make the final payment and find yourself debt-free.

Finding the right repayment strategy helps you stick to it and increases your chances of success.

BEWARE OF PREPAYMENT PENALTIES
When paying your debt off too quickly can actually hurt you

You've got a little extra cash, and the best thing you can do is pay off that lingering debt, right? Not so fast—if your lender charges a prepayment penalty, a fee for paying off too much debt too quickly, making early payments can be more costly than beneficial. You may see prepayment penalties in some auto or personal loans, but the place you're most likely to come across prepayment penalties is in mortgages.

How Prepayment Penalties Work

Prepayment penalties vary from lender to lender. Some penalties are a fixed amount. Others are set as a percentage of your remaining balance, or as a certain number of months' worth of interest. When it comes to mortgages, the amount charged may also depend on how long the mortgage has been in place, though the period in which prepayment penalties may be charged rarely extends beyond five years.

Refinancing a mortgage can also trigger a prepayment penalty. Some prepayment penalties, known as "hard prepays," also penalize borrowers for selling their home too soon after signing the mortgage.

Let's look at an example: Say you take out a $350,000, 30-year mortgage with an interest rate of 4.5%. It also has a prepayment penalty of six months' interest that kicks in if you pay off more than 20% of the loan in any of the first three years.

If you decide to refinance after two years, the prepayment penalty will be assessed, and you'll owe your lender six times the monthly interest, which comes out to around $1,250 x 6, or $7,500. That's a pretty hefty fee, and one you likely want to avoid.

Why Lenders Charge Prepayment Penalties

It may seem counterintuitive for lenders to assess a penalty for paying back a loan too fast. After all, don't lenders want their money? The answer is yes, but they also want to profit off the interest that accumulates on your loan. If a mortgage is paid off in two or three years—or if the borrower sells or refinances the home after two or three years—the lender collects less interest than they would during the full life of the loan. Prepayment penalties protect lenders against the possibility they will lose out on interest collections.

Weigh Prepayment Penalty Clauses Carefully

Borrowers should be cautious about prepayment penalties, but they shouldn't necessarily avoid signing a contract that includes one. Often, lenders include prepayment penalties in mortgages with lower-than-average interest rates. If you're relatively certain you won't sell or refinance your house too soon after entering into a mortgage, it may be worth the risk of a prepayment penalty to nab that low rate.

Prepayment penalties can make paying off debt early a costly move.

Side gigs can help you pay off your debts more quickly.

INCREASING YOUR INCOME TO PAY DOWN DEBT
A side hustle can put you on the path to success

Paying off debt is a lot easier when you have some extra income to work with, but your regular paycheck may be a static number that's not likely to grow, especially in the short term.

If you're committed to paying off your debt quickly, consider pursuing a side gig on top of your main source of income. This secondary job might be closely related to your current career or it could be a welcome change of pace. Use it as an opportunity to explore your different work options. If you've always worked for someone else, you can see what it's like to be your own boss. If you're tied to your desk in your 9-to-5, you can try a job that gets you on your feet.

Not only is an extra source of income good for your wallet now, but it could also set the stage to provide you some extra cash during retirement. You may start by moonlighting or working weekends or you may consider taking on a few more hours and boosting your cash flow when you retire from your day job. Here are some side jobs to consider:

● **Join the Gig Economy** One of the perks of the gig economy, which relies on independent contractors instead of full-time staff employees, is doing as much or as little work as you want, on your own schedule. Turn your set of wheels into a money-making machine by giving rides, making deliveries or running errands through companies including Lyft, Uber, Instacart and Postmates. If you have a specialized skill, such as graphic design or web coding, use it to start a freelance business. Check out TaskRabbit to take on odd jobs like painting, repairs, cleaning and other chores.

● **Teach, Consult or Coach** You've spent years collecting knowledge that has helped you in your personal and professional life. As a teacher or consultant, you can parlay that expertise into a second act. Work in the classroom as a substitute teacher, or one-on-one as a tutor. Develop a course on the subject you know best and offer it online through Skillshare, then offer consulting and coaching services to your students. If you'd prefer to get away from the desk, try coaching or refereeing kids' sports. Or if you know how to play an instrument, teach music lessons.

● **Learn a New Skill** Become a florist, baker or barista. Don't be deterred by a job you've never done before. Lots of companies provide on-the-job training, and your new skills could open the door to more opportunities.

● **Turn Your Hobby Into Cash** Knitting, ceramics or woodworking may have been an activity just for your own enjoyment in the past. But you might find a market for your arts and crafts when you start your own shop on Etsy, where shoppers are looking for unique, handcrafted goods. If you'd like to downsize your collection of vinyl records or classic books, consider becoming a seller on eBay or Amazon.

• **Get a Retail Job** Stock shelves or work as a cashier at your favorite grocery store or bookstore. If you love camping, fishing or outdoor sports, share your tips on the sales floor of a sporting goods store. Pick a store where you shop often—and enjoy the perks of an employee discount.

• **Be a Friendly Face** Many businesses need part-time workers in guest services, a position that's ideal if you love chatting and making people feel welcome. Try working the front desk at a museum, health club or spa. Or share your local knowledge as a hotel concierge.

• **Head for the Outdoors** If mowing lawns is your meditation, work on the grounds crew for a golf course or your city parks. Or offer your services to neighbors and local small businesses.

• **Become a House-Sitter** Pick up the mail, water the plants and keep an eye on things when your neighbors are gone. Offer your services as a caretaker who keeps the house safe, clean and functional while owners are away.

• **Tackle Administrative Tasks** You may have already picked up the key skills needed for office work, like data entry, billing and working a phone system. Check hospitals and colleges for departments that are often hiring, or browse online job postings to become a virtual assistant.

• **Work With Pets** If you have a way with animals, try walking dogs or pet-sitting for friends and neighbors whose pets are alone while they're at work or on vacation.

Be diligent about using your extra cash for repayment, and your debt may disappear before you know it. Once it's gone, you can ditch the side gig for free time—or start putting your extra income toward savings.

WHAT TO DO WITH A WINDFALL

You finally did your taxes and the results are in: You're getting a sizable refund from Uncle Sam. But before you start scheming about buying a new TV or taking yourself out to celebrate, consider how you can use that windfall to pay off some debt.

Anytime you receive a large chunk of money outside of your regular income—whether it's through the lottery, as an inheritance or as a gift—at least some of it should go toward debt. You'll get maximum benefit from your extra cash, because it will save you from paying interest over time.

If you have a variety of debts, look at what you currently owe and the interest rates for each. Try to pay down the debt with the highest interest rate first. This helps prevent that debt from continuing to grow at a faster rate than your other debts. If you can pay it off completely, great. If you still have some of that windfall left to put toward another debt, even better.

Some people believe that they'll ultimately do better by investing their money and letting it grow, rather than simply using it to pay down debts. Sometimes that's true, but if you have a credit card balance with an 18% APR, you'll be hard-pressed to find an investment that can yield those kinds of returns. Not only that, using your windfall to pay down debt is a sure bet. Investments—especially ones with potentially high returns—can be risky.

Regardless of how much of your windfall you use to pay off debts, the important thing is to use your extra money wisely to get yourself onto stable financial ground. While that newly freed-up credit may feel like it's burning a hole in your pocket, beware of falling back into bad spending habits that could put you right back where you started.

Using side income to pay down debt will also give your credit a step up.

Turn hobbies into paying gigs—that way you can do the things you enjoy while reducing your debt.

CREATIVE WAYS TO SAVE TO PAY DOWN DEBT

Sometimes, decreasing your spending is easier than increasing your income. Even if you already live on a pretty tight budget, there are probably ways you can still cut back. If you've already ditched your latte habit and traded in your gym membership for daily runs in the park, it might be time to get a little more creative with your saving.

Start a Lunch Club You know that eating out is a big no-no when you're trying to save, but busy schedules don't always allow for the amount of planning necessary to pack a lunch each day. Try forming a lunch club with co-workers. Pick one day of the week that each person is responsible for bringing the lunch. Planning becomes a lot easier when you're only responsible for meals once a week.

Buy in Bulk Sure, it feels like you're saving money when you only spend a dollar at a time to buy one roll of toilet paper. But when you buy a package of 24 or 36 rolls, you can save big per unit. Food staples like rice, flour and dried beans can also be far less expensive when bought in bulk. Calculate what you're saving by buying in bulk and put that toward your debt.

Volunteer Volunteering is unpaid, but it often comes with perks. If you're an avid runner but want to save on race fees, see if you can put in volunteer hours in exchange for a bib. Theater lover? Volunteer to usher and see the show for free. Music festivals, sporting events and museums can be costly, but often offer free admission for a little of your time.

Make Gifts Instead of Buying Them "It's the thought that counts," right? If your loved ones know you're working hard to save, they'll understand when you don't break the bank for birthdays. Homemade crafts or treats accompanied by a heartfelt card are sure to be well-received and can feel more meaningful than something bought in a store.

WHAT NOT TO DO WHEN PAYING OFF DEBT
There are many wrong ways to tackle debt

Paying off debt isn't always easy. But using the right strategies can make clearing out debt a lot easier. Similarly, knowing what not to do when paying down debt can be just as critical. Here's a look at some common missteps to avoid when managing your debt.

Accumulating More Debt

It's hard to make your debt smaller if you keep adding to it. So don't spend your evening building a get-out-of-debt plan only to pull out your credit card at the mall the next day.

Also, think twice before taking out new lines of credit to pay off debts. While it may be tempting to wipe out a bunch of account balances with a new loan, this strategy can backfire. For instance, when you replace your credit card debt or past-due bills with a home equity loan, you're raising the stakes by putting your home up as collateral. If you default, you risk losing your house. Also, some debts, such as medical expenses, don't accrue interest. Replacing those with a loan is bound to cost you more in the long run.

Borrowing Against Your 401(k)

The purpose of your 401(k) is to shore up your future retirement. It can only fulfill that purpose if the money actually stays there, accruing interest. The government wants you to save for retirement, so it allows your savings in these plans to take advantage of tax-deferred growth. Your money can continue to grow year after year tax-free, and you only will owe taxes on your savings and earnings once you start making withdrawals when you reach retirement age.

Borrowing from your 401(k) is a costly endeavor. Not only is the money you borrow no longer building your savings, you will have to pay interest on the loan. While that interest is ultimately paid back to you, it will be taxed double. You repay the 401(k) loan with after-tax dollars, and that money will be taxed again when you withdraw it in retirement.

If you leave your job before you've repaid the loan, you will have only a few months to repay it in full. If you don't repay it, the balance of the loan will be considered a distribution, and you'll have to pay taxes on that amount—plus a 10% penalty if you're younger than 59½. Resist the temptation to dip into your 401(k) and you'll be thankful once you retire.

In fact, rather than borrowing from a 401(k), it can make good financial sense to keep contributing to your 401(k) up to your employer-match amount as you pay off your debt. Matching funds are effectively a 100% return on your investment, which you may want to prioritize over making extra payments to certain debts.

Avoid taking on new debts so you don't hurt the progress you make paying off the old ones.

Forgoing an Emergency Fund

Though it may be tempting, draining your emergency fund to accelerate your debt payments can cost you in the long run. Without that rainy-day money on hand, the next emergency car repair or out-of-pocket medical expense could send you deeper into debt. Keeping a store of cash to pay unexpected expenses is an important element of your debt-repayment plan.

Falling for a Debt-Relief Scam

Debt relief scams lure people with large credit card debt by offering to intervene with creditors to negotiate a lower debt obligation. Be wary of services that charge large up-front fees. In the end, customers may get little or nothing in return. Before accepting the services of a firm that promises to help you with your debt, do a web search of the company's name along with "scam" or "lawsuit" to see if there are any known issues. You can also search for the company at the Better Business Bureau website.

Closing Your Credit Accounts After You Pay Them Off

One of the key factors in your credit score is your credit utilization—the amount of your total credit you're using. By reducing the amount of credit you have available, you cheat yourself out of some of the benefit of having paid down your debt. Unless you find you can't resist using your credit cards when they're available, the best way to repair your credit is to keep your accounts without using them.

Doing Nothing

It's easy to become so overwhelmed by the size of your debt that you lose the motivation to make a repayment plan and stick to it. You may not even know where to begin—the debt with the lowest balance or the one with the highest interest rate? Don't let yourself be paralyzed by inaction. The truth is that any plan is better than no plan—so pick one and start chipping away. Your future self will be glad you did.

Watch out for debt-relief scams that promise to lower debt on your behalf—but for a big fee.

139

HOW PERSONAL BANKRUPTCY WORKS A look at which debts it erases, and which will remain

Sometimes a person can become so overwhelmed by debt that there is simply no way to get out from under it. Personal bankruptcy laws are designed for these extreme circumstances, providing relief to the debtor while protecting creditors where possible. But it can't erase every kind of debt, and it comes at a steep cost to your credit score.

A personal bankruptcy almost always falls into one of two categories: Chapter 7 or Chapter 13. Here's a closer look:

Chapter 7

When you file for Chapter 7 relief, you settle your dischargeable debts through liquidation. In other words, you sell off your assets and distribute the proceeds to your creditors. However, some or all of your personal property may be exempt from liquidation, meaning you get to keep it.

● **Eligibility** To be eligible, your monthly income must fall below the state median, or you must demonstrate that your effective monthly income is lower than it seems. You also must show proof that you've been to credit counseling.

● **What Kinds of Debt It Can Discharge** Several types of debt, including alimony, child support, certain taxes, government loans and fines for injuries or death caused by drunken driving cannot be discharged by a Chapter 7 filing without paying them in full.

Secured debts, such as a mortgage or auto loan, can be discharged through Chapter 7, but not without losing the collateral property. That means you can only discharge a mortgage by giving up your home, and you can only discharge an auto loan by giving up your vehicle. Be sure to seek legal counsel to determine that your debts can be discharged.

● **How to File** You file for Chapter 7 bankruptcy by filing a petition, along with several required pieces of financial information, with your local bankruptcy court. There is a fee to file, but the court may allow you to pay in installments or waive the fees altogether.

The appointed bankruptcy trustee will convene a creditors' meeting, or a "341 hearing," which gives creditors a chance to ask you questions under oath. In practice, creditors don't usually show up.

Once you file, the property you own—barring most pensions and educational trusts—goes into the "bankruptcy estate." This includes items you've given away recently, income and dividends from your property, your stake in any marital property, inheritances received up to six months after filing, intellectual property and stock options. The bankruptcy estate is then used to pay off creditors.

PRO TIP

A bankruptcy filing can drag down your credit. Chapter 7 is erased from your report after 10 years; Chapter 13 takes seven years.

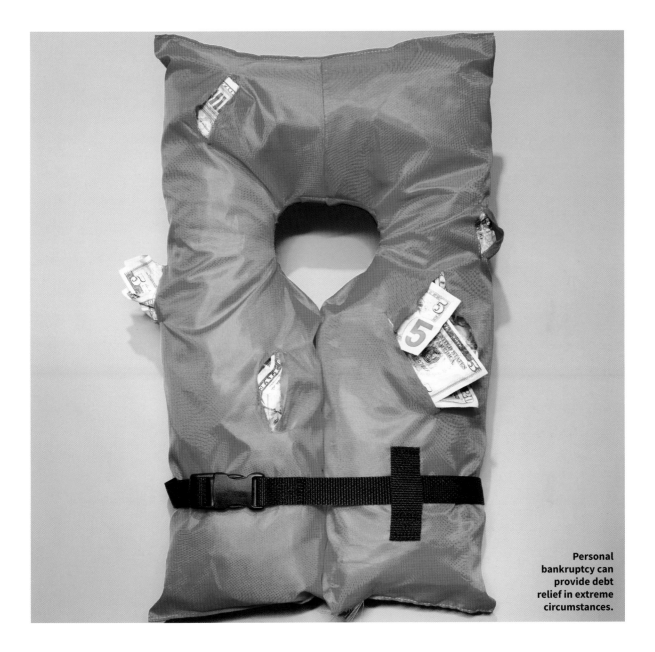

Personal bankruptcy can provide debt relief in extreme circumstances.

You can exempt certain necessary assets from the bankruptcy estate by including claims in your initial filing. It's not uncommon to file a no-asset bankruptcy, in which the debtor has no nonexempt property that the trustee deems worth selling, and the applicable debts are discharged without the debtor liquidating anything. In either case, the debts are usually discharged approximately two to three months after the creditors' meeting.

Chapter 13

If you receive a steady paycheck, then Chapter 13 can be a way for you to clear debts by paying off all or part of your delinquent accounts over a three-to-five-year repayment plan. Chapter 13 is appeal-

Filing for personal bankruptcy will impact your credit rating for years to come.

As long as you continue to make regular payments, you remain protected from foreclosure and repossession under Chapter 13 bankruptcy.

ing because, as long as you continue to make your payments, you're protected from foreclosure and repossession, giving you a chance to save your home or vehicle.

Another benefit of Chapter 13 is that you make just one monthly payment to a trustee, who then distributes the money to each of your creditors.

• **Eligibility** You can file under Chapter 13 if you are an individual who makes more than enough money to cover living expenses and debt payments, and the size of your secured and unsecured debt falls below certain thresholds.

Chapter 13 bankruptcy can discharge debts covered by Chapter 7, as well as recent tax penalties and certain divorce-related debts. But even if you can't discharge a debt through Chapter 13, you may still be able to use the repayment period to recover from delinquency by making current required payments.

• **How to File** Filing for Chapter 13 is similar to filing for Chapter 7, though the fees to file are slightly smaller, and there's an extra hearing where you include a proposal for repayment. If it's confirmed—and you stick to your repayment plan—all your dischargeable debts will be wiped clean.

If during the course of repayment you find you no longer need Chapter 13 protections, you can freely dismiss your bankruptcy. If, on the other hand, you're unable to make the payments, you can convert the bankruptcy to Chapter 7.

DEBT

Staying Out
of Debt

Strategies for breaking free of your bills

THE BENEFITS OF BUDGETING You wouldn't run a business without a budget, so why run your life without one?

Sitting down to make a budget isn't many people's idea of a good time. But then again, neither is scrambling to pay your bills at the end of every month.

For many people, budgets are only for when money is tight. After all, if you need to make a budget, it must mean there's not enough money for everything you need, right? Wrong. Budgeting is for everyone. No matter how much you have now, it's still important to plan for the unexpected *and* for the future. Not only that, budgeting helps protect against lifestyle inflation when you get a raise or a new job. And it can also help you get and stay out of debt.

Budgets help keep spending in perspective and make it easier to stick to your financial plans.

Make One Decision, Not Lots of Decisions

PRO TIP

Here and there, small expenditures might not feel like much in the moment. But over time they can add up to major financial headaches.

When you make a budget, you're deciding to prioritize your long-term financial goals—whether that's saving for retirement or simply having something set aside for emergencies. It's a big decision that saves you from making lots of small (and potentially costly) decisions on a daily basis. For example, an invitation from friends to try out a trendy new restaurant can be tough to turn down in the moment. But if your budget doesn't include money for dining out, the decision has already been made for you. Turning down the invite may feel momentarily disappointing, but you'll ultimately feel better for having stuck to your plan and prioritizing the things you've decided are important.

Without a Budget, You Have No Control

Have you ever looked at your bank statement and thought, "That can't be right. Where'd all my money go?" When we don't have a budget, our spending adds up without us realizing it. That's

Regularly setting a
budget helps you
pinpoint just where
your money goes.

because small expenditures here and there don't feel like much in the moment. But over the course of a month, a $5 daily expense—like a sandwich at the lunch cart—adds up to $150 monthly. That's $150 that could have gone to an emergency fund, a retirement account or to pay down debt—all of which you're likely to get more long-term benefit from than a couple dozen BLTs.

Without a budget, you also risk not having enough money to pay your bills at the end of the month. When that happens, it's all too easy to reach for your credit cards—adding to your debt and potentially creating a cycle that's difficult to escape. Not only does this perpetuate bad spending habits, it also means that when an emergency hits, you won't have the savings to cover it, and could end up in even more debt. In the long term, it can mean not having enough saved to fund a comfortable retirement.

Budgeting for the Win!

Budgeting is difficult because it conflicts with our desire for instant gratification. But the long-term benefits are huge—especially if you have a specific financial goal in mind, such as retiring by a certain age, or saving for a down payment on a house. Unless you have a sudden windfall—and how many of us can actually count on that?—it can be extremely difficult to fund those goals without a solid plan.

Keep your budget realistic and plan for any needs both current and those that might be forthcoming.

The good news is that budgeting doesn't have to be painful. You can still enjoy yourself and spend money, even when you have a long-term goal in mind. You just need to make sure your budget is realistic and accounts for your needs both now and later. If dining out with friends is important to you, you can allow for that—just make sure you set a monthly limit and stick to it. There's no point in making a budget if you'll regularly break your own rules.

Once you make—and get into the habit of adhering to—your budget, you'll probably find yourself far less stressed when it comes to money. That's because you'll know what's coming in and what's going out. So even when you do have to say no to some things, the control you'll gain over your financial life will likely feel well worth the cost.

Who doesn't want a nest egg? A budget can help you build one.

HOW TO BUILD A BUDGET

Creating a budget doesn't have to be complicated. Put simply, it's a process that involves calculating how much money comes in and how much goes out. By comparing the two, you can make more informed decisions about where your money goes. Here's how to start building a budget that works for you.

Figure Out Your After-Tax Income

Generally, that's whatever your paychecks add up to each month. If your employer takes out money for health insurance or a 401(k), take note of how much. You'll factor those numbers in later.

Calculate Any Additional Income

If you receive alimony or make money as an independent contractor, estimate how much you make each month. If that money is taxable (meaning you'll be expected to report it and pay taxes on it), deduct a percentage to cover the taxes. Finally, add that total to your other income.

Calculate Your Expenses

Start with the necessities: rent, utilities, child care, groceries and anything else you can't do without. Be careful not to confuse needs with wants. For example, do you really need cable bundled with your internet package?

TIP If your employer takes out money for health insurance or a 401(k), you can note that here. For example, if your employer deducts $240 per month for health insurance, that's a necessary expense. But make sure you also count that $240 as income (even though it was taken out of your paycheck). That way, you're not budgeting for health insurance twice.

Subtract Your Needs From Your Income

Let's say your monthly income totals $3,200. When you add up your mortgage payment, your phone bill, transportation and any other necessities, you get a total of $1,400. Subtract the cost of necessities ($1,400) from your total income ($3,200). You're now left with $1,800.

TIP Many personal finance experts recommend the 50/30/20 style of budgeting. This type of budget allots 50% of your income for needs, 30% for wants (such as travel, dining out and entertainment) and 20% for savings and debt repayment. While this may not be possible, depending on your income and expenses, it's a good rule of thumb to keep in mind.

Allow for Wants

Determine how much you want to allow yourself for extras each month—whether that's dining out, travel, or a fancy gym membership—and subtract that from what you have left after you've taken care of your necessities.

TIP Look over your last few bank statements and note how you've been spending money.

For instance, are you comfortable spending $100 each month for ride shares, or would you rather commit to public transportation and put that $100 toward something else?

Save

Once you've deducted both your needs and your wants, make sure there's something left for savings. If your budget is particularly tight, or if you're working to aggressively pay down debt, this can be tough. But make sure you put something toward an emergency fund or a long-term savings account. Even if it's a small amount, you'll thank yourself later.

TIPS FOR LIVING A DEBT-FREE LIFE While small daily expenses add up, it's those big decisions that make or break long-term goals

Living completely debt-free isn't always possible. If you want to buy a home or pay for college, chances are you'll need to take on some debt. However, there's plenty of debt that can be avoided.

Making smart money decisions can help you stay on budget and avoid taking on more debt. As you figure out strategies that work for you, don't neglect these three major components of the debt-free lifestyle.

Buy (or Rent) an Affordable House

Americans' housing costs are on the rise. While financial experts recommend keeping your housing costs at no more than 30% of your income, many people spend significantly more to keep a roof over their heads. As your housing costs creep closer to 40% or 50% of your income, digging out of debt becomes much harder—as does saving for future goals, such as retirement or a child's college tuition.

If finding less-expensive housing is impossible in your area, there may still be ways to reduce your monthly payments. For example, consider downsizing or getting a roommate to help you cut costs. If you're a homeowner, you may be able to refinance your mortgage for a better interest rate, or look for more affordable homeowner's insurance. Anything you can do to keep your housing costs down will go a long way to creating a debt-free life.

Keep an Emergency Fund

No matter how stable things seem right now, life happens. One bad illness can keep you out of work for weeks. Or maybe your car's transmission quits or your home's roof springs a leak. While many people keep a credit card handy for emergencies, it's always better to have cash on hand. With an emergency fund, you can pay for the unexpected without racking up debt and having to pay interest on it.

To build an emergency fund, start by saving whatever you can. Your goal should be to save enough to cover three to six months' worth of basic living expenses, like housing, transportation, insurance, phone and food. Keep that money in a safe, accessible place, like a savings account, and decide ahead of time what constitutes an emergency—so you won't be tempted to use it unless absolutely necessary.

Avoid Lifestyle Inflation

For many of us, when we get a raise, we start spending more. This phenomenon is known as lifestyle inflation. While making more money should allow you to live more comfortably and spend a little more freely, it's also important to make sure your savings—and debt repayment—grow proportionately to your income. Before you start planning a luxury vacation, make sure you're continuing to budget for savings and a debt-repayment plan. Those are choices that will benefit you over the long term.

Make sure you grow your savings and debt-repayment budgets alongside your earnings.

HOW TO MAKE SMARTER DAY-TO-DAY MONEY DECISIONS Six simple habits that can supercharge your debt-reduction efforts

Whether you're working to pay down debt or celebrating making the last payment on your credit card balance, there's one more item on your to-do list: avoiding taking on new debt. Building an emergency fund will help, as will being smart about how you pay for housing and other big items on your personal balance sheet. But the daily money decisions you make also matter.

After all, most people don't go into debt all at once. Instead, debt usually grows out of a large number of small decisions. Examining those decisions and building better habits can help generate big savings over time.

Find Out Where You Spend Your Money
Many bad spending habits develop subconsciously. If you don't know how much you spend on any given activity, you don't know what to change. Keeping track of your spending doesn't even require the same level of commitment as setting and sticking to a budget. Go through your bank statements and tally up the areas where you spend the most. If your bank offers online banking services, you may be able to get this information with a few clicks of the mouse. Once you identify those areas, develop targets for reducing your spending patterns. For example, if you spend a lot of money on groceries, remind-

ing yourself of that fact while you're in the store could be enough to improve your shopping savvy.

Trim Your Automatic Payments
Automatic payments have a way of taking place out of sight and out of mind. That can make for wasteful spending habits that you don't even recognize. To knock out those passive expenses, scour a year's worth of credit card statements for recurring payments to services you no longer need, from gym memberships to magazine or app subscriptions. When you find something you don't need or use anymore, cancel it right away. That way you won't forget about it until it automatically renews.

The daily decisions you make about money can add up to big savings.

Put Your Savings on Autopilot

The same convenience that makes automatic subscriptions easy to forget about makes automatic savings a great idea. Think of savings like any other bill or expense and prioritize it accordingly. Setting up a periodic automatic transfer so part of your paycheck goes directly into a savings or investment account makes saving that money your default behavior—and reduces any temptation to spend it instead.

Develop a Meal Plan

Eating out is convenient, but it also can be expensive. Instead, make a plan for how often you'll eat in and eat out. For instance, you might decide to take lunch to work four days a week and eat out only on the fifth day. Planning ahead for meals can also keep your grocery list better focused on the ingredients you need, helping you avoid the urge to buy pricey premade or processed foods.

Be Patient and Shop Around

Beware of impulse buying. Every dollar you spend on an unintended purchase is a dollar that can't be put to use elsewhere. If you run into a must-have item, remember that you don't have to buy it immediately. Look for items that are on sale, cut coupons, and compare prices at multiple retailers, both online and in store. With patience, you may find that you get a better deal—or decide you don't really need that item in the first place.

Be Persistent

For most people, debt grows over time. If you don't go into debt overnight, don't expect to get out of it overnight, either. Good spending habits take time and practice to build, and nobody's perfect. You may run into setbacks, but if you keep an eye on your spending habits and make a concerted effort to change them, the savings will follow.

Setting up a
periodic automatic
transfer so part
of your paycheck
goes directly
to a savings or
investment account
makes saving
that money your
default behavior.

**Savings and debt
both grow over time,
so you'll need to be
patient and persistent
to make a change.**

SIMPLE WAYS TO SAVE MORE

Money saving habits you develop now can also help you reduce the need to borrow in the future. Here are some tips to help build your savings.

Bank Your Raises When you receive a raise or a big year-end bonus, consider using the bump in your paycheck to increase your savings or contributions to your 401(k), individual retirement account or health-savings account.

Trim Your Utility Bills Monitor your energy and water use and look for ways to cut back. It could be as simple as raising the A/C in the summer or lowering the thermostat in the winter. A few degrees can make a big difference in your savings in a year's time.

Put Off Pricey Purchases Do a little research when you're in the market for a big-ticket item, then wait for sales or times of the year when retailers are slashing prices. You'll find great discounts on TVs around the Super Bowl and new lawn mowers at the end of summer.

Sell What You're Not Using Websites like eBay, Craigslist and Gift Card Granny provide the virtual equivalent of a garage sale, allowing those unused gift cards, clothing, furniture and baby gear to move on to a second life, while you pocket some extra cash.

Put Yourself on a Spending Diet Challenge yourself to go a set number of days or weeks without buying clothes or making the splurge of your choice—perhaps dining out or making any other nonessential purchases. At the end of your self-imposed spending fast, allocate that unspent cash to savings. Try doing this on a regular basis, say once a month.

Take Advantage of Discounts If you're a student, a member of the military or a senior, use discounts to trim your spending. Ask around at restaurants, movie theaters, museums, amusement parks, grocery stores, salons and other businesses. Some may offer discounts even if they don't prominently advertise them.

Lower your energy bills by setting a timer on your thermostat.

Automatic savings plans make it easy for your money to grow over time.

TRAIN YOUR BRAIN How to harness your brain's natural tendencies to stay out of debt

We all know how easy it is to overspend. But why does sticking to a budget feel like it takes a will of steel? The answer lies in our behavioral biases—the subject of much research by scientists who study why we act the way we do. Thanks to their research, we can actually understand why we overspend and why it's difficult to commit to a savings plan. We can also use these techniques to make better financial decisions.

> Our brains can have a hard time staying motivated. If you're working toward a long-term goal, like paying off a mortgage, it's easy to lose sight of the big picture over time.

Set Small Goals

Our brains can have a hard time staying motivated. If you're working toward a long-term goal, like paying off a mortgage, it's easy to lose sight of the big picture over time.

By setting incremental goals along the way, you can increase your motivation, celebrate small wins and help ensure success. Short-term goals (and the corresponding rewards when you reach them) are great tools for staying motivated. For a long-term goal like getting out of debt, start by choosing a mini-goal that you can realistically reach within a few months—maybe paying off one of your credit cards, or putting an extra $1,000 toward the principal on your mortgage. When you meet your mini-goal, reward yourself. Then look for the next incremental goal that will take you another step closer to your final destination.

Make It Visible

One problem with debt is that it's not visible to us—until we open our monthly bills. And when something's not fresh in our mind, we tend to let it slip. Keep a visible reminder of your debt somewhere that you'll notice it, such as on your desk or the fridge. Make sure it can change over time as your debt decreases. You can use a simple solution like a white board where you mark down your debt monthly, or you can get creative. You can make a paper chain to signify your debt (and eliminate one link every time you make a payment) or stick up Post-It notes for each kind of debt you have and take them down once they're paid off. Seeing a visual representation of your debt on a regular basis will keep it in the forefront of your mind, making you more likely to stick to your repayment plan.

Say Your Vows

Making a verbal commitment to pay off a debt—whether to a friend or to your lender—can signifi-

Examine your finances carefully to be sure you aren't leaving money on the table somewhere.

cantly increase your chances of succeeding. One study showed that delinquent credit card users were more likely to make a payment if they committed over the phone to making a payment on a specific day. For larger goals, finding a finance buddy is a great way to hold yourself accountable. Ask a trusted friend or family member to check in with you regularly about your debt repayment and savings. If they truly have your best interests at heart, they'll want to encourage you, while making sure you don't back down from your goals. Of course, there are also apps available to help you track—and even curb—your spending. They may lack the human touch, but they also never sleep.

Have a System

Making a plan can help keep the emotion out of our decision-making processes. That's why systems for organizing and tracking debt payments—such as the avalanche method or the snowball method—can be such powerful tools. Experts agree that without a system, you're likely to lose track of your budget and long-term plan. You also won't have a reliable way to track your progress and reward yourself for following through. There's no single plan that's right for everyone; choose one system and run with it. If you find it's not working, don't give up—just try another plan until you find one that fits.

Minimize Temptation

Identify what spurs you to overspend. For example, if you know that idle moments at your desk lead to frivolous online shopping, download an app to help you block the websites that hit you hardest. If having cash in your wallet means you'll immediately spend it, don't leave the house with a stack of $20s. And if your finances are stable enough, try automating your savings. Choose a reasonable amount, and have your bank transfer it into savings each month. If your employer offers matching contributions to a 401(k), be sure to take maximum advantage of that, too. By making that money magically disappear from your checking account each month, it won't be sitting around tempting you to spend it—instead, you'll be banking it for a rainy day.

Find the right budget-tracking system that works for your personality and lifestyle.

THE IMPORTANCE OF AN EMERGENCY FUND
Save for the unexpected to avoid going into debt

W e've all been taught that it's important to save for a rainy day. Yet more than 60% of Americans don't have enough in savings to cover even a $1,000 emergency. So when the furnace needs replacing or the car breaks down, how are you going to pay that bill?

One option is to pull out your credit card. But an emergency charged today on your credit card could take years to pay off. It can also be tempting to tap into retirement savings through plans such as IRAs and 401(k)s, but withdrawing that money prematurely can mean a big chunk of it goes toward paying taxes and penalties.

An emergency fund can provide you with the savings you need to deal with life's curveballs without digging into debt or jeopardizing your other savings plans.

PRO TIP

An emergency fund should be easy to access, like a savings account. If it's tied up in stocks or assets, it's not liquid enough.

Building an Emergency Fund

Ideally, your emergency fund should be large enough to cover between three and six months' worth of living expenses. You don't need enough for absolutely everything—just enough to cover necessities such as housing, food, utilities, transportation and regular debt repayments. If you don't have steady employment, or if a new job could be difficult to come by, you may want to save more than six months' worth of expenses.

Keep your emergency fund in an easily accessible place, such as a bank savings account. You also may consider stashing your savings in a money market account or a short-term bond fund to earn some additional interest. But the goal is to be able to quickly access your savings, so focus more on liquidity than the interest rate your savings will earn.

Stick to a Strategy

Remember that building an emergency fund can take time. Look for opportunities to add to your fund on a regular basis. For instance, you may be able to set up an automatic transfer of a portion of each paycheck into a savings account. Also consider funneling part of your year-end bonus or your income tax refund into your emergency fund. Together, those regular and occasional contributions will add up.

You don't need to set aside your other savings goals in order to get your emergency fund up and running. Instead, you can divide your cash among your savings goals—secure in the knowledge that you're making progress toward all of them at the same time.

Best of all, you don't need to reach your goal of having three to six months' of savings before your emergency fund can come in handy. Saving just $100 per month will leave you with $1,200 at the end of the year. And while that may not be enough to live on for three months, it can definitely help cover life's little emergencies.

Keep an emergency fund set aside for an unexpected crisis.

GETTING HELP Consider debt counseling for support in taking control of your finances

Paying off debt can feel like a lonely and overwhelming endeavor. Whether you're falling further behind on your debts or struggling to keep current with your payments, you may benefit from a helping hand. Resources such as debt-counseling services can help you take control of your finances.

What is Debt Counseling?

Debt counseling, or credit counseling, is a service to help consumers who can no longer manage their debt. Debt counselors may educate their clients, assist with monthly budgets and help design a long-term plan to rein in their debt. The companies are often nonprofits that have agreements with creditors to suspend collection efforts and late fees as long as you follow the agreed-upon repayment plan.

These rules may not apply to secured debts, such as your mortgage or auto loan, but a debt counselor can still advise you on how best to avoid foreclosure or repossession. A debt-counseling agency will consider your whole financial picture—bills, expenses, debts and income—and help you design a budget that keeps you above water. It may also offer free workshops and educational materials, and help you get copies of your credit reports. Most urgently, it can help you create a repayment plan, possibly with lower monthly payments, for debts you've fallen behind on.

Debt Counseling vs. Debt Settlement

Debt counseling should not be confused with debt settlement (or "debt relief"). Debt-settlement companies frequently charge you high fees to pressure your creditors into settling your debts for less than what is owed. This situation sounds good on the surface. Who doesn't want to save money? But a settlement can actually severely damage your credit.

Debt counselors, on the other hand, are professionals with your best interests at heart who can help you develop a plan for bringing your debt under control. Weed out any firms that promise to eliminate or reduce your debt for an up-front fee. Some reputable debt counselors charge fees, but never before they've actually delivered results for you.

> Debt counseling is very different from debt relief companies—the latter charge high fees and can impact your credit rating.

PRO TIP

Debt counselors are professionals who can help you develop a plan for bringing your debt under control and keeping it in check for the long term.

Debt counseling can help you get control of your debt and protect your credit score.

How Debt Counselors Lower Payments

There are two straightforward ways credit-counseling agencies lower your monthly payment: by securing a lower interest rate on a debt or credit account or by extending the term of the loan. The first method will save you money in the long run, while the second can cost you more in interest payments. Either choice might make it possible to get out from under your debt without resorting to bankruptcy or debt settlement.

What Is a Debt Management Plan?

When a debt counselor negotiates lower monthly payments for your debts, it's typically part of a "debt-management plan." Under such a plan, you make a single payment to the credit-counseling agency—usually either every month or every paycheck—and the agency passes the money along to your creditors.

Choosing a Reputable Credit-Counseling Agency

Most credit-counseling agencies are nonprofit organizations, but that status is not a guarantee of reliability. The National Foundation for Credit Counseling and the Association of Independent Consumer Credit Counseling Agencies are two organizations that provide accreditation to debt-counseling firms. Choose an accredited agency to reduce the chance that you'll be taken advantage of by predatory debt-settlement agencies.

PRO TIP

A good debt counselor will typically look for ways to reduce your monthly payments, but he or she won't negotiate with your creditors.

In general, you should avoid organizations that charge for educational materials, are vague about their counselors' qualifications or pay their employees based on how many of their services they convince you to sign up for.

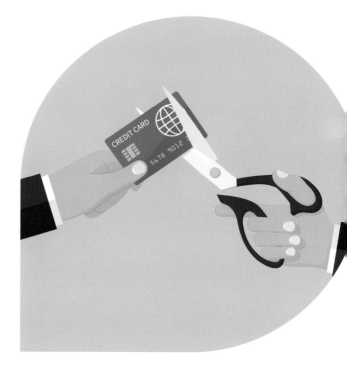

Have Realistic Expectations

Debt counseling can be a lifesaver, but it's not a magic wand. A good debt counselor will typically look for ways to reduce your monthly payments to help you stay on top of your finances, but he or she won't negotiate with your creditors to reduce the total amount you owe.

That's usually a good thing in the long run. Simply using debt-counseling services and following the payment plan you work out with them will show up on your credit report, but those activities won't have much effect on your score. Debt settlement, on the other hand, can have a more severe impact on your credit, especially if a debt-settlement agency advises you to stop paying your debts as a negotiating tool.

Think Long-Term

Setting up a debt-management plan can feel like a desperate scramble to get current with your debts, but the goal is bigger than that. Ultimately, you want to avoid finding yourself in this situation in the future. And that's exactly what a good debt counselor is there to help you with.

A good debt counselor can help you establish a long-term plan for getting your finances in order.

SECTION

09

Workbook

Hands-on tools to help you
track and manage your debt

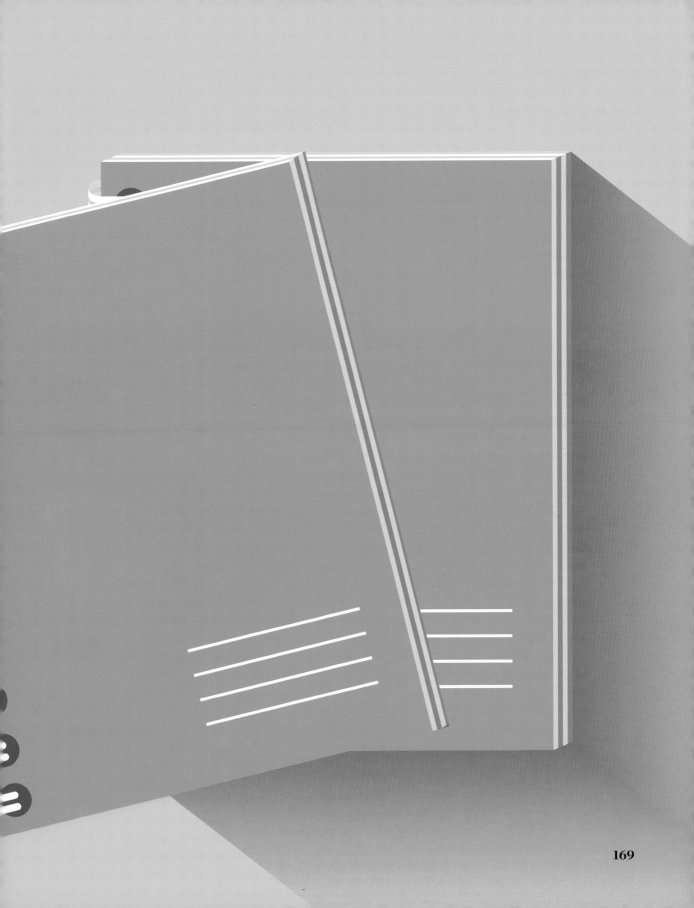

DEBT REPAYMENT PLAN

Debt can be daunting, but taking small steps to pay it off can help you free up money to save for an emergency fund or reach other savings goals

The first step is getting real about how much debt you have. Use this worksheet to list all your debt, including your mortgage, credit cards, home equity, auto loans and student debt.

Once you have it all down on paper, you can map out a strategy for tackling it. Aim to pay the minimum on all your debt except for one. Put extra money toward that targeted debt. Then, once you've paid it off, you can roll that payment into the next debt on your list.

You'll pay less in interest over time if you focus on paying off the highest-interest debt first. But you may find it inspiring to knock off the debt with the lowest dollar amount first.

DEBT	Interest Rate	Loan Balance	Monthly Minimum Payment	Extra Payment	Date Paid Off
	%	$	$	$	
	%	$	$	$	
	%	$	$	$	
	%	$	$	$	
	%	$	$	$	
	%	$	$	$	
	%	$	$	$	
	%	$	$	$	
	%	$	$	$	
	%	$	$	$	
	%	$	$	$	
	%	$	$	$	
	%	$	$	$	
	%	$	$	$	
	%	$	$	$	

AVALANCHE METHOD WORKSHEET

The avalanche method of tackling debt focuses on paying off your highest-interest rate loans, saving you money in the long run by knocking out the most costly debt first

Put as much money as you can toward your debt with the highest interest rate, while making minimum payments on the rest. Once it's paid off, put that same amount of money toward your next-highest-rate debt. Repeat until all debts are paid.

Use this worksheet to put the avalanche method into action. Determine how much money you can put toward paying down your debt each month. Then review your debts, listing them from highest interest rate to lowest, and making note of the minimum payment for each one. Once all minimum payments are made, put any leftover money toward the loan with the highest-interest rate. Cross off debts as you pay them off and focus on the next debt on the list.

Monthly Debt-Repayment Budget: $

DEBT	Interest Rate	Balance	Minimum Payment	New Payment
Example: Debt 1	% 14	$ 700	$ 25	$ 25 + balance of debt repayment budget
Example: Debt 2	% 10	$ 900	$ 35	$ 35
	%	$	$	$
	%	$	$	$
	%	$	$	$
	%	$	$	$
	%	$	$	$
	%	$	$	$
	%	$	$	$
	%	$	$	$
	%	$	$	$
	%	$	$	$
	%	$	$	$
	%	$	$	$

SNOWBALL METHOD WORKSHEET

Use this worksheet to put the snowball method into action

Here, you'll put as much money as you can toward paying off your smallest debt first. Determine your monthly debt-repayment budget. List your debts from smallest to largest balance. Pay the minimums on all of your debts, then put the rest of that budget toward your smallest balance.

Once the smallest debt is repaid, take the entire amount you were paying—both the minimum payment and the extra cash you added—and put it toward your next-smallest debt. Like rolling a snowball down a hill, the more debts you pay off, the more powerful the next payment becomes.

Monthly Debt-Repayment Budget: $

DEBT	Amount Owed	Minimum Payment	Snowball Payment
Example: Debt 1	$ 700	$ 20	$ 20 + the rest of your debt repayment budget
Example: Debt 2	$ 1,000	$ 30	$ 30
	$	$	$
	$	$	$
	$	$	$
	$	$	$
	$	$	$
	$	$	$
	$	$	$
	$	$	$
	$	$	$
	$	$	$
	$	$	$
	$	$	$
	$	$	$
	$	$	$
	$	$	$
	$	$	$

BUILDING A BUDGET

Reaching your financial goals requires planning and intentional action

Creating a spending plan by budgeting your monthly income and expenses can help you move closer to your goals. Following a budget helps you prioritize your spending needs, ensures you have enough money to cover your expenses and can help you get out of or avoid debt.

Use this budgeting worksheet to create a plan and start managing your money better.

INCOME SOURCE

	Amount	
	$	
	$	**Gross Monthly Income Total**
	$	$

BILL OR EXPENSE

	Amount	Due	Paid
	$	$	
	$	$	
	$	$	
Total	$		

Total Income	Total Expenses	Extra to Debt	Extra to Savings
$	$	$	$

IDEAS FOR GENERATING EXTRA INCOME

You've made your budget, calculated your income and expenses and want to pay down your debt even faster. Here's a plan

There are only two ways to generate extra money in your budget—cut expenses or increase your income. If you've cut your expenses as much as you can, then generating extra funds to put toward outstanding balances may be the missing link to paying down your debt.

From picking up extra hours at work to tutoring or teaching another skill or purging your clothes or unused items and selling them online, there are many ways to generate extra income. Put this worksheet somewhere visible in your home and keep the ideas flowing.

IDEAS

DEBT-TO-INCOME RATIO

Lenders use your debt-to-income ratio (DTI) to help them determine how much debt you're carrying and whether you can handle it

Your front-end DTI is the percentage of your gross income spent on recurring housing debts, such as rent or mortgage payments. Your back-end DTI is the percentage of your gross income that is spent on all debt payments, including student loans, auto loans, credit cards and child support or ali-mony. Recurring expenses like auto insurance or utility bills don't count. A healthy front-end DTI is 28% or less, and a healthy back-end DTI is 36% or lower. Lenders may look at both when determining whether to loan you money.

Determine whether you are in a healthy range by calculating each of these debt-to-income ratios

FRONT-END DTI

Total Monthly Housing Expenses = $ _____

Divided by

Gross Monthly Income (Before Taxes) = $ _____ **X 100 = Front-End DTI Percentage**

BACK-END DTI

Total Monthly Debt Expenses = _____

Divided by

Gross Monthly Income (Before Taxes) = _____ **X 100 = Back-End DTI Percentage**

DEBT RESOURCES

From student loans to medical bills, debt can feel overwhelming. If you find yourself in a position of not being able to pay, or not knowing where to start, there are organizations you can turn to for help.

Credit-Counseling Organizations

These organizations can advise you on managing your money and debts, and may even offer free educational resources and workshops.

• The United States Trustee Program keeps a list of credit-counseling agencies approved to provide pre-bankruptcy counseling.
Visit *justice.gov/ust/credit-counseling-debtor-education-information*

• You can also find certified credit counselors through the National Foundation for Credit Counseling and the Financial Counseling Association of America.
Visit *nfcc.org, fcaa.org*

• The Federal Trade Commission and the Financial Literacy & Education Commission both offer a wealth of information about managing your personal finances and getting out of debt.
Visit *ftc.gov, mymoney.gov*

Before doing business with any credit-counseling agency, check their background and review information such as licensing status. Review customer complaints with your state attorney general's office or a local consumer protection agency.

Medical Debt

If you're facing large medical bills, determine what you can afford to pay each month and discuss a payment plan with your hospital's billing department. Nonprofit hospitals are also required to provide financial assistance to qualified low-income patients.

IRS Debt

If you can't afford to pay the taxes you owe, there may be payment options available to you.

• The IRS offers payment plan options.
Visit *irs.gov/payments/online-payment-agreement-application*

• Some consumers can also qualify for an offer in compromise, meaning that the IRS will settle the tax debt for less than what is owed. To qualify for an offer in compromise, the IRS reviews your ability to pay, which includes income, assets and expenses.
Visit *irs.gov/payments/offer-in-compromise*

MORTGAGE COMPARISON WORKSHEET

It's not just about how much home you can afford—it's what kind of mortgage you can afford

Before buying a home, most people spend plenty of time shopping around, looking for a good deal that suits their needs. After all, for many of us, a home is the largest purchase we'll make in our lifetimes. But the decision-making doesn't end when you decide on a house. You'll also want to shop around to find the mortgage that's best for you. Use this worksheet to compare how your different mortgage options stack up:

	Mortgage 1	Mortgage 2	Mortgage 3
Name of Lender			
Name of contact			
Contact's phone			
Mortgage amount			
Loan term			
How often can the interest rate change?			
Initial interest rate			
Highest potential interest rate			
Initial monthly payment			
Highest potential monthly payment			
Origination, application and broker fees			
Can any of these fees be waived?			
Other closing costs (title search, transfer taxes, etc.)			
Will the lender set up an escrow account for taxes and insurance?			
What will the monthly escrow payment be?			
Total initial monthly payment (including escrow)			

DETERMINING EQUITY

How much equity do you have in your home or car? And what does that really mean?

Equity is a way of expressing how much of something you own outright. Sure, when you buy a house with a mortgage, you technically own that house. But until that mortgage is paid off, the bank can lay claim to it if you fail to make your payments.

Knowing how much equity you have in a house or car helps you understand what you can expect if you want to sell it. For homes, it can also help you calculate how much you may be able to borrow in a home equity loan, should you need to.

CALCULATING EQUITY IN A HOME

Appraised market value of your home _____

(minus)

How much you still owe _____

(equals)

Total equity _____

Most lenders want you to have at least 20% equity in your home before they'll extend a home equity loan. But their decision ultimately is determined by a range of factors beyond your equity, including your credit score and debt-to-income ratio.

To calculate the percentage of equity you have, divide your equity by your home's appraised market value:

[equity] _____ / [value] _____ = _____% equity

Calculating equity in a car

Calculating equity in a car is different than calculating it for a home. While borrowers have historically expected their homes to go up in value over the course of a mortgage, cars lose value, or depreciate, over time. That makes it easy to find yourself down the line having negative equity in a car—meaning you owe more than the car is worth. Calculating the equity in your vehicle can help you determine whether it makes financial sense to sell or trade in your vehicle. Start by getting an estimate of your car's value. Good resources for calculating the value of a used car are Edmunds and Kelley Blue Book. But keep in mind, many factors can contribute to a car's real market value, including the popularity of the model, the number of miles and even the condition of the interior.

CALCULATING YOUR EQUITY IN YOUR CAR

How much your car is worth   _____

(minus)

How much you owe on your car   _____

(equals)

_____

If you have positive equity in your car, you may be able to trade it in at a dealership or sell it and take home some cash.

However, if you have negative equity, you likely still owe money on your car even after selling or trading it in.

UNDERSTANDING YOUR CREDIT REPORT

Your credit score can have a huge effect on your life. But many people don't know their credit score, or how to check it. Your credit score is a product of your credit report, which lists detailed information about your income, debt and payment history. Any time you apply for a loan or a credit card, the lender uses your credit report to decide whether to approve your application, how much credit they'll offer and the terms of the loan.

So before walking into a lender's office, take a few minutes to figure out your credit score and take a look at the latest copy of your credit report. Also, knowing what's on your credit report can help you improve your credit score by showing you areas where you can improve.

How your FICO Score is Calculated

• **Payment History** This is often the most important part of your score's calculation. It looks at whether or not you make your payments on

time. Generally, credit bureaus look at payments on debts—mortgages, credit card payments, auto loans. Payments for things like rent, utilities and cell phone bills don't usually affect your credit score—unless you've been so delinquent that they've been sent to collections.

• **Utilization** How much of your current credit are you using? For example, your score may suffer if you are using $4,800 of your $5,000 line of credit. But if you're only using $1,000 of your credit, you look like a safer bet to lenders.

• **Length of Credit** The longer you've had an account, the more a lender can know about your history. If all of your credit cards were opened in the last six months, your score might not look as good as if you'd had those cards for several years.

• **Recent Activity** This includes recent applications for credit and any major use of your credit in a short period of time. Lenders like to see a person whose behavior they can predict, and applying for a bunch of cards at once, or maxing out your credit in a short amount of time, can be a red flag.

- **Mix of Credit** Having a variety of accounts can also help your credit score. For example, having a mortgage, a credit card and an auto loan shows that you're able to make regular payments on a variety of debts.

Tracking your Score Over Time

Today, most credit cards offer the opportunity to check your credit score for free through their websites. Your credit score can change at any time, depending on how you use your credit. Try checking it over the course of a month, and then over the course of several months.

Use this area to track your credit score

Week 1	
Week 2	
Week 3	
Week 4	
Month 1	
Month 2	
Month 3	
Month 4	

Checking your Credit Report for Free

Each of the three main credit bureaus (Experian, Equifax and TransUnion) are required by law to offer you one free credit report per year. The Federal Trade Commission offers three ways you can request a free credit report:

- Visit www.annualcreditreport.com
- Call 1-877-322-8228
- Or fill out the FTC's Annual Credit Report Request Form and mail it to:
  Annual Credit Report Request Service
  P.O. Box 105281
  Atlanta, GA 30348-5281

While Experian, Equifax and TransUnion each also offer access to credit reports through their websites, the FTC does not recommend contacting the individual bureaus directly.

Some websites focused on finance (such as NerdWallet) offer services to access your credit report for free more often, so you can check your report monthly, or even more frequently than that.

Correcting Errors on your Credit Report

Credit reports sometimes have errors. These mistakes can negatively affect your ability to qualify for a loan or a credit card. To correct these errors, follow these steps:

Step 1 Submit your complaint to the appropriate credit bureau in writing. If you need help drafting a letter, the FTC's website (www.consumer.ftc.gov) offers sample letters that you can customize for your situation. Include with your letter copies of any documentation that helps prove your claim.

Step 2 The credit bureau must then investigate your claim (generally within 30 days) and provide you with a report documenting the results of the investigation. They'll also provide you with a new, free credit report based on their findings.

Step 3 If the bureau finds that there was an error on your credit report, you may request that they send your revised credit report to anyone who received your report in the past six months or to anyone who received your report for the purposes of employment within the last two years.

Step 4 You can also tell the information provider (the person or business that reported the item to the credit bureau) that you dispute their claim. Do this in writing and provide copies of documentation to support your claim. If they continue to report the disputed item, they must also inform the credit bureaus of your dispute.

BUILDING AN EMERGENCY FUND

You know you need to put money away for a rainy day. But just how much should you have saved to patch that roof?

When the unexpected happens, an emergency fund can help you avoid slipping into debt. But it can take a concerted effort to put away enough savings for a healthy emergency fund. Experts suggest saving three to six months' worth of basic living expenses. But that doesn't mean the amount you would normally spend for those months. Rather, it refers to how much you spend on the basics—things like rent, food and transportation.

Use this worksheet to calculate how much you should aim for in your emergency fund and how long it will take you to save that up.

EXPENSE	Monthly Cost	Cost for three months	Cost for six months
Housing (rent or mortgage)	$	$	$
Food	$	$	$
Transportation (including car insurance)	$	$	$
	$	$	$
Debt repayment (student loans, car payments, etc.)	$	$	$
	$	$	$
Health insurance	$	$	$
Phone	$	$	$
Other	$	$	$
	$	$	$
	$	$	$
	$	$	$
	$	$	$
	$	$	$
	$	$	$
	$	$	$
Total	$		

In a worst-case scenario, your emergency fund can help you cover these basic expenses should you lose your job or be unable to work for any reason. But most often, people use their emergency funds to cover unexpected costs that they can't cover with their regular income.

See how many of these common expenses your potential emergency fund could cover:

Average cost of: $

Car repair	$500-600
Emergency room visit	$1,400
Veterinary service	$800 - $1,500
Repair a water heater	$100 - $1,150
Replacing a phone or laptop	$530 - $1500

Once you've determined how much you want to save, you'll need a plan for doing so. Set a goal, along with a timeline for reaching it. Depending on your budget, it may take you a while to get there.

But every month you'll be closer to your goal.

Emergency Fund Savings Goal _____

Figure out how much you'll need to save each month to meet your goal. Divide your goal number of months you'll take to reach it.
For example:

To save $3,600 in 12 months: $3,600 / 12 = $300 per month.

**To reach _____ in 6 months,
you'll need to save _____ per month.
To reach _____ in 12 months,
you'll need to save _____ per month.
To reach _____ in 18 months,
you'll need to save _____ per month.**

Once you determine how much you'll put toward your emergency fund each month, you'll need to figure out where that money will come from. Assuming you already have a budget, look over line items that you can afford to cut back on.

Then, figure out how much you can cut from each:

BUDGET ITEM	Monthly Spending	Amount to move	New monthly spending
Dining out	$	$	$
Shopping	$	$	$
Entertainment	$	$	$
Other	$	$	$
Other	$	$	$

CARS: BUYING VS. LEASING

Which is the smarter choice? It depends on your needs.

Owning a car can feel great. You're always ready for the open road. But are you also ready for the hefty repairs it's sure to need down the line? For some people, leasing a car provides all of the convenience of car ownership without many of the headaches. But like many things, the right choice for you will depend on your finances and your lifestyle. Take a look at the pros and cons of each to see which works best for you:

	Buying	**Leasing**
PROS	Living without car payments once the car is paid off	Often lower monthly payments than a car loan
	Ability to customize your car	Always driving a new car
	Not responsible for fixing cosmetic damage if you don't want to	Not responsible for long-term maintenance
	Ability to sell car whenever you want	Little money needed up front
	Drive as many miles annually as you want to	Allows you to drive a more expensive vehicle than you could afford to buy
	Option to trade the car in at a dealership	Option to buy the car during the lease
CONS	Responsible for all repairs	Always having a monthly payment
	Car depreciates in value over time	Paying more over the long-term than buying
	Larger down payment necessary for purchase	Annual cap on mileage, with fees for overuse

If the primary factor in your decision to buy or lease is how much you'll spend on a car, use this worksheet to calculate what your costs are likely to be:

BUYING

Cost of car _____

Additional fees _____

Auto loan interest rate _____

Down payment _____

Monthly payment _____

Length of loan _____

Total amount paid at end of loan* _____

* Use an online tool such as Bankrate's Auto Loan Calculator, which factors the loan's interest rate into the final calculation.

LEASING

Length of lease _____

Down payment _____

Monthly payment _____

Additional monthly fees _____

Total amount paid at end of lease [down payment + (monthly payment and fees x length of lease)] _____

It's likely that the total amount of the lease is significantly less than the total cost of buying a car. However, look at the numbers. Your car loan may take five years to pay off, while your lease only lasts for three years. Not only that, the car you purchased will hopefully have some resale value at the end of the loan, so you can recoup some of the cost.

For example:

Even if you paid $30,000 total for a new car, once it's paid off, you may be able to sell that car for $14,000—meaning you really only paid $16,000 in total.

COVER malerapaso/Getty Images **FRONT FLAP** Peter Dazeley/Getty Images **SPINE** ilbusca/Getty Images **2-3** malerapaso/Getty Images **4** (From left) Monkey Business Images/Shutterstock; Anatolir/Shutterstock **5** (From top) Geber86/Getty Images; twomeows/Getty Images **6-7** Lightspring/Shutterstock **9** Maskot/Getty Images **10-11** sorbetto/Getty Images **12** WindAwake/Shutterstock **13** Mint Images/Getty Images **15** sorbetto/Getty Images **16** mangsaabguru/Shutterstock **17** Maskot/Getty Images **19** Damir Khabirov/iStockphoto **20** Caterina Bernardi/Tetra images RF/Getty Images **21** Tony Tallec/Alamy Stock Photo **22** Adam Gault/Getty Images **23** AndreyPopov/Getty Images **24-25** Westend61/Getty Images **26** Sentavio/Getty Images **28** ImageFlow/Shutterstock **29** FaberrInk/Getty Images **31** Monkey Business Images/Shutterstock **33** RomoloTavani/Getty Images **35** Cecilie_Arcurs/Getty Images **36** RedlineVector/Shutterstock **37** Monty Rakusen/Cultura RF/Getty Images **38** Alexandr III/Shutterstock **39** claudenakagawa/Getty Images **41** REDPIXEL.PL/Shutterstock **42** sorbetto/Getty Images **43-44** Paul Bradbury/Getty Images (2) **45** sorbetto/Getty Images **47** Haali/Shutterstock **48** PeopleImages/Getty Images **49** Iryna Kalamurza/Shutterstock **50** TarikVision/Shutterstock **52** sorbetto/Getty Images **53** SolStock/Getty Images **54** sorbetto/Getty Images **56** pixdeluxe/Getty Images **57** Westend61/Getty Images **59** KrizzDaPaul/Getty Images **60-61** Gigonthebeach/Shutterstock **63** Andy Dean Photography/Shutterstock **64-65** Mark Edward Atkinson/Tracey Lee/Tetra images RF/Getty Images **67** Denphumi/Shutterstock 68 megaflopp/Getty Images **69** sorbetto/Getty Images **70-71** Tony Tallec/Alamy Stock Photo **72** sorbetto/Getty Images **73** PeopleImages/Getty Images **74** Vladimir Vladimirov/Getty Images **75** Rawpixel.com/Shutterstock **76-77** kate_sept2004/Getty Images **79** sureeporn/Getty Images **81** TarikVision/Shutterstock **83** Alex_Doubovitsky/Getty Images **84** Nicescene/Shutterstock **85** Barry Diomede/Alamy Stock Photo **86-87** MangoStar_Studio/Getty Images **89** garagestock/Shutterstock **90** Helen Cortez/EyeEm/Getty Images **92** PeopleImages/Getty Images **93** robuart/Shutterstock **94-95** Ariel Skelley/Getty Images 96 seamartini/Getty Images **98** drogatnev/Getty Images **99** Nastasic/Getty Images **101** filmfoto/Alamy Stock Photo Tetra images RF/Getty Images **102-103** Maksym Povozniuk/Shutterstock 105 stefanamer/Getty Images **106** Don Farrall/Getty Images **108-109** sorbetto/Getty Images (2) **110** Tetra images RF/Getty Images **111-113** PM Images/Getty Images (2) **115** greyj/Getty Images **116** emmgunn/Getty Images **117** Infadel/Getty Images **118-119** Sean Gladwell/Getty Images **120-121** Anatolir/Shutterstock **123** sorbetto/Getty Images **125** SERGII IAREMENKO/Science Photo Libra/Getty Images **127** jovan vitanovski/Shutterstock **129** sorbetto/Getty Images **130** cjp/Getty Images 133 sorbetto/Getty Images **134-135** Camille Tokerud/Getty Images **137** Rob Lewine/Tetra images RF/Getty Images 138-139 Rawpixel/Getty Images **141** Shana Novak/Getty Images **142-143** VectorMine/Shutterstock **144-145** sorbetto/Getty Images 146 Tim Platt/Getty Images **147** JGI/Jamie Grill/Tetra images RF/Getty Images **148** Andy Roberts/Getty Images **149** Andrey_Popov/Shutterstock **151** pathdoc/Shutterstock **152** PM Images/Getty Images 153 damircudic/Getty Images **154-155** PM Images/Getty Images **156** Matt_Brown/Getty Images **157** sorbetto/Getty Images **159** PM Images/Getty Images **160** twomeows/Getty Images **161** Nattakorn Maneerat/EyeEm/Getty Images **162-163** TAW4/Getty Images **165** Image Source/Getty Images **166** hvostik/Shutterstock **167** Geber86/Getty Images **168-169** Be.sign/Shutterstock **173** TarikVision/Shutterstock **176** JGI/Jamie Grill/Tetra images RF/Getty Images **178** malerapaso/Getty Images **179** manusapon kasosod/Getty Images **180** vladwel/Getty Images **184** joruba/Getty Images **BACK FLAP** (Sand, umbrella, coconut) Alessandro De Carli/EyeEm/Getty Images (Pig, chair, ball) DNY59/Getty Images **BACK COVER** malerapaso/Getty Images

SPECIAL THANKS TO CONTRIBUTING WRITERS

Erin Heger, Matthew Kuhrt, Andrew Palmer, Donna Sellinger,
Emily Smith, Param Anand Singh, Andy Vantrease

CENTENNIAL BOOKS

An Imprint of
Centennial Media, LLC
40 Worth St., 10th Floor
New York, NY 10013, U.S.A.

ISBN 978-1-951274-25-2
Distributed by
Simon & Schuster, Inc.
1230 Avenue of the Americas
New York, NY 10020, U.S.A.

For information about custom editions, special sales and premium and corporate purchases,
please contact Centennial Media at contact@centennialmedia.com.

Manufactured in China

Publishers & Co-Founders Ben Harris, Sebastian Raatz
Editorial Director Annabel Vered
Creative Director Jessica Power
Executive Editor Janet Giovanelli
Deputy Editors Ron Kelly, Alyssa Shaffer
Design Director Ben Margherita
Art Directors Natali Suasnavas, Joseph Ulatowski
Production Manager Paul Rodina
Production Assistant Alyssa Swiderski
Editorial Assistant Tiana Schippa
Sales & Marketing Jeremy Nurnberg